Dancing Bears

BOOK C

by
Hilary Burkard
& Tom Burkard

Stories illustrated by
Ed McLachlan

First published 2001, Promethean Trust
Second Edition 2002, Promethean Trust
Third Edition (Revised) 2004, Hilary Burkard
Fourth Edition (Revised) 2005, Hilary Burkard
Fifth Edition (Revised) 2006, Hilary Burkard
Sixth Edition (Revised) 2014, Hilary Burkard

Copyright © Hilary Burkard 2014

All rights reserved. No part of this publication may be reproduced or transmitted in any form or by any means, electronic or mechanical, including photocopying, recording, or any information storage or retrieval system, without the written permission of the publisher.

ISBN: 9781905174355

PUBLISHED BY HILARY BURKARD

DISTRIBUTED BY
SOUND FOUNDATIONS
www.soundfoundations.co.uk
sales@soundfoundations.co.uk
☎ 08448 708158 FAX 08448 708172

Dancing Bears C

Contents:

The Ground Rules 4
The Teaching Techniques 5
-are, -ire 9
food, school, choose, shoot, soon, room, word, worth, work ... 15
-le, pure, cure, sure 21
dead, head, bread, read, early, learn, war, warm 24
giant 26
-are, -ire; Longer words 30
pretty, goes, does, trouble, double, people, idea, poor 33
Dropping the 'e' 38
-ion 48
ready, instead, heavy, healthy, heard, search, warning 51
guess, guest, guitar, guard, guide, guilty, sign 59
pirate 61
Soft 'c' 67
door, floor 70
'y' to 'i' 84
thought, ought, bought, fought, busy, great, break 87
-ure 92
quiet, keys 97
young, country, couple, touch, laugh, build, built 104
rough, tough, enough, eight, police 112
moustache 114
-age 119
bear, wear, tear, swear, lie, tie, die, pie 122
Soft 'g' 127
ph, hard 'ch' 136
fruit, juice, suit, cruise, bruise, island 139

Dancing Bears C — Introduction:

The **Sound Foundations** philosophy:

As a teacher, your objective is to get your pupil to make the maximum number of correct responses—*and* the fewest errors—in the available time. If you manage to do this, you can't go far wrong.

The Ground Rules:

1. **Teach—don't test.** Whenever a child gets stuck, say the sounds for them or tell them the word. Do not force them to 'work it out for themselves'. You do not want to make reading into a struggle.

2. Do not give ticks for a 'good try'. Just practise it and go back to it the next day.

3. Keep the lesson going at a cracking pace! Do not let your pupil's attention wander.

4. Daily lessons are essential. You only need to find 10 minutes per day for each slow reader.

The Teaching Techniques:

All pupils *must* complete either Dancing Bears Books A and B or Fast Track Book AB before starting this book.

Although Book A and the beginning of Fast Track may seem very easy for pupils who have already made a start in reading, it is part of a carefully planned sequence.

1. **Using the flashcards**—oddly enough, this can be the hardest part! If you did not grow up playing card games, just handling the cards can be tricky. Be sure you read the instructions carefully.

2. **Using the cursor**—This is quite easy to learn. The cursor trains the child to read from left to right, and it trains them to look at every letter in a word.

3. **The 'Flashback' technique**—After you have corrected an error, you must return to the same item again.

All this is explained on the following pages. Please read them carefully.

The Flashcards—it is not enough just to 'know' the letter-sounds. If the response is not instant and automatic, your pupil will not be able to concentrate on sounding out words. You must practise the flashcards *every* lesson while using **Dancing Bears**.

By the time you start Dancing Bears C, your pupil should have had all the flashcards introduced. There are only two new flashcard sounds in Book C but your pupil may still need to practise some sounds that were introduced towards the end of Book B.

Whenever your pupil gets a sound wrong, just tell him what the sound is, and then put the card behind the next one. **Never, ever** make a big deal of it. The whole point of **Dancing Bears** is to make reading easy. If a pupil does not say the right answer straight away, you simply tell him what it is—and then ask him to repeat it.

When do I stop using the flashcards?

When the pupil can say the sounds quicker than you can flip the flashcards then you can stop practising those cards. Do not be tempted to stop using the flashcards too soon. Children must be able to respond instantly and automatically to the flashcards, otherwise, they will have trouble blending. You must "practise past the point of perfection." And no—your pupils will not get bored: children love getting it right!

Using the cursor:

A cursor is a piece of card about the size of a business card with a small notch cut out of one corner. You must use the cursor at all times.

1. When your pupil is sounding out a word, you can reveal one sound at a time. For example, the word shark has three sounds—*sh...ar...k.*

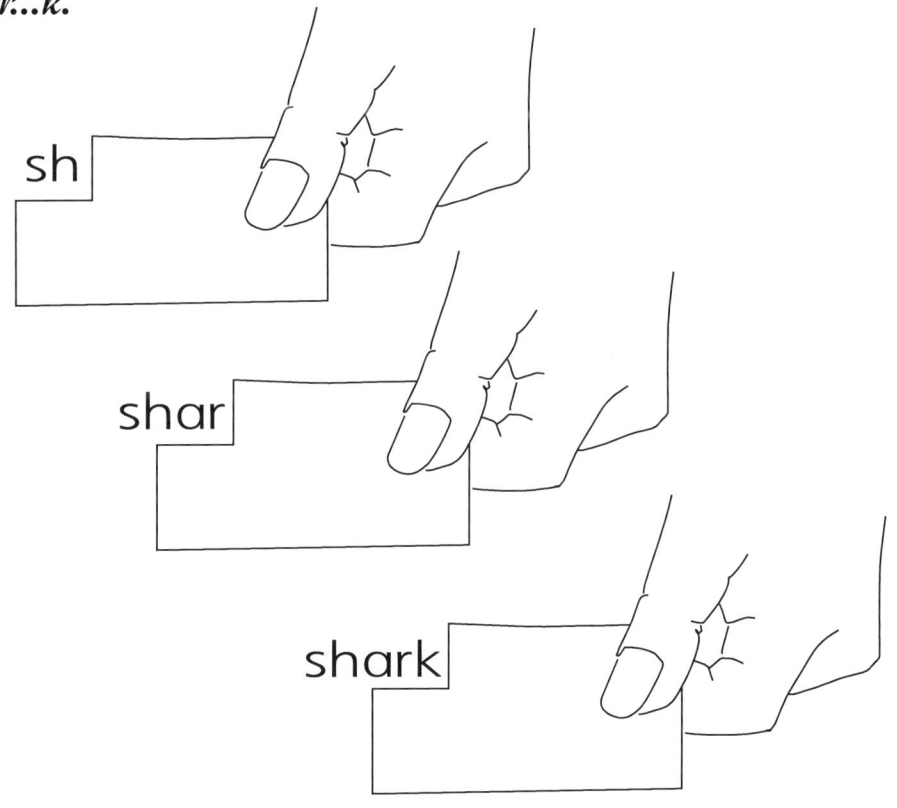

2. When your pupil already knows a word, just move the cursor smoothly and quickly across the letters. Never sound out words if you do not have to.

3. If your pupil makes a mistake, you can back up the cursor and then sound out the word.

The cursor eliminates visual confusion. When children have been taught to read whole words, their eyes often jump all over the place, trying to scramble the letters to make a 'fit' with a word they know.

If you use the cursor, it is highly unlikely that your pupil will need coloured overlays or tinted glasses.

The Flashback Technique—is used every time a pupil makes an error. If you go back to the instructions for using the flashcards, you will see that when a pupil has forgotten a card, you tell him what it is and then put it behind the next card. That way the card comes up again while it is still fresh in his memory. This is an example of the Flashback Technique.

You will also use the Flashback Technique when a pupil is reading words. Whenever a pupil fails to read the word:

- correct him
- get him to repeat it
- go on to the next item
- go back to the one he just missed.
- When you have finished a line, go back again to any words missed.
- When you have finished the exercise for the day, go back over all words missed again.

This way, the pupil will usually earn his tick for the line the next day. (Remember—you never tick a line when the pupil gets it right on the second go—you must wait until the next lesson.)

The Teaching Environment—Always teach your pupil in a quiet room with no distractions. Do not let him bring toys or mobile phones with him.

Always sit facing your pupil. It is very difficult to use the cursor effectively if you are sitting side-by-side. You need eye contact. When you are facing your pupil it is easier to see when he is confused or getting tired. You can step in right away and show him what to do before he makes a mistake and loses confidence.

-are, -ire

Remember to practise the flashcards every day.

care	bare	stare	dare	fare	☐
share	scare	wire	spare	hire	☐
aware	dire	rare	square	tire	☐

I don't care what Paul told you to do. ☐

My mum only gave me the bus fare to get home. ☐

You will get a shock from that bare wire. ☐

Did Maud hire a new car? ☐

Don't you dare try to scare your little sister! ☐

I told Dawn that it is rude to stare at strangers. ☐

| hare | mare | fire | snare | spire | ☐ |
| flare | glare | mire | pare | shire | ☐ |

Would you care to share those prawns with both of us? ☐

Our bay mare gave birth to a frisky foal. ☐

The hunter caught a hare in a snare. ☐

Spike might not like the glare of those bright lights. ☐

If you are cold you can light a coal fire in the grate. ☐

It rained so hard that our mare got stuck in the mire. ☐

Maud saw some rare jewels in the bank vault. ☐

Dancing Bears C

Decoding Power Pages:

These exercises are the 'secret ingredient' of **Dancing Bears**. All good readers can decode letters to sound, even if they have never seen the word before. This is how good readers learn new words.

When children read the words on the Decoding Power Pages, they should not be trying to find a 'match' with a word they know. All the words on Decoding Power Pages are regular—they can all be 'sounded out' without any guesswork. Some of the words are very unusual, like 'quern', 'bort' and 'loach'—but they are all real words.

Remember—you must always use the cursor. You must teach pupils to scan from left to right, and to read every sound.

Do not give a tick for a 'good try'. Your pupil must get all the words on a line right, without any help, to earn a tick

If your pupil cannot remember all the sounds or cannot blend them, say the sounds yourself and let him say the word. If he is in a total muddle, model the whole process, and then get him to repeat it. Always go back to any word you helped with—see **The Flashback Technique** on page 8.

DECODING POWER PAGE

If your pupil makes a mistake, back up the cursor and then sound out the word.

preshrunk	squirted	shredded	thrilling	☐
bare	wire	hare	fire	☐
blue	fewer	cruel	strewn	☐
hire	pare	tire	share	☐
duke	code	hate	pile	☐
squawked	respray	splitting	scratchy	☐
rare	dire	square	squire	☐
awful	saucer	tawny	gauze	☐
brew	skewer	cruelest	refuel	☐
mire	mare	spare	spire	☐
sprawling	because	deploy	decant	☐
spurn	range	vice	skirmish	☐
shire	glare	quire	scare	☐
jaunty	applause	lawful	audit	☐
sire	tire	stare	ware	☐
describe	scruffy	thrice	splinter	☐
flare	mire	snare	spire	☐
pew	gruesome	ensue	fluently	☐

Dancing Bears C

Word building:

Most pupils like these exercises because they discover that reading long words is not really all that difficult once you know the building blocks or morphemes.

Most of the examples start off with a real word but there are some that start with a part of a word such as *cept* or *struct*. These are always in italics. Some morphemes have more than one syllable.

The only difficult items are the ones where the syllable structure changes in the middle of the line, these are marked with a star in the exercises. For instance:

rel   relate   *relative   relatively

Note that in speech, 'relate' breaks up as *re-late,* whereas 'relative' works out as *rel-uh-tive*. With words like this, you will probably have to tell your pupil the correct response the first time round. Do not forget to use the Flashback Technique.

With the cursor, segment the root word into phonemes as usual. Then with each successive word use the cursor to reveal each morpheme as a whole.

Wordbuilder

Do not award ticks for a 'good try'—your pupil will pay for it later!

chain	chained	unchained	☐
pay	repay	repaying	☐
load	upload	uploaded	☐
mark	market	supermarket	☐
new	renew	renewal	☐

Sue unchained a shopping trolley at the supermarket. ☐

You will be repaying that loan until next June. ☐

Prue uploaded a new file. ☐

Dawn's books are due for renewal on Tuesday. ☐

cork	uncork	uncorked		☐
nove	*renove*	renovate	renovating	☐
pert	expert	expertly	inexpertly	☐
tract	distract	distracted		☐
pair	repair	repaired		☐
count	discount	discounted		☐

Maud just uncorked a jug of fine white wine. ☐

I was going to wash the dishes but Jake distracted me. ☐

Paul repaired my bike expertly. ☐

I am beginning to tire of renovating this chair. ☐

Has that store discounted the price of new blue jeans? ☐

Dancing Bears C

Cloze Sentences:

Pupils enjoy these exercises and they get to practise using the words they have learnt by reading them in meaningful sentences.

In the box at the top of each page, you will find the new words that the pupil will need in order to read the sentences. Most are exception (tricky) words or words with ambiguous digraphs. Move the cursor smoothly across the letters while saying the sounds in the word. If your pupil gets confused, point out which sounds are regular and which are tricky. If he cannot read the word, model the correct response, then use the Flashback Technique (see page 8) and repeat each word until firm.

Reading the sentences:

For this exercise you will need a blank sheet of thin card about A6 in size. Cover the sentence and ask the pupil to read the three 'answer' words underneath the sentence first, using the cursor as usual. (This is to prevent him guessing at the missing word.) Then let the pupil read the sentence, still using the cursor. If the pupil reads the sentence and selects the right answer without prompting, circle the correct word. (The pupil **should not** write the word—this takes too long and is a distraction.) Otherwise, the sentence should be repeated in a subsequent lesson. If the pupil does not know the meaning of a word, explain it as simply as possible—but in no circumstances encourage pupils to guess at words they have read incorrectly.

food, school, choose, shoot, soon, room, word, worth, work

My older sisters have to _____ a bedroom.
snore   shire   share

The bay mare is the best _____ we have.
horse   house   hare

Do you know how much those rare jewels are _____ ?
word   worth   work

You will need some matches to light the _____ .
fare   fir   fire

They put up a barbed wire fence around the _____ .
farm   food   churn

The fish shop will hire anyone who wants to _____ .
sleep   steal   work

Your mum packed all your spare socks in the _____ box.
squid   square   squawk

Please don't _____ me—I didn't cook the school dinners.
share   shoot   soon

15

Dancing Bears C

Fluency Reading:

Timed readings will help your child read words quickly and automatically. The times are very easy at first. Some children get nervous when they are being tested so try not to let the stopwatch worry them. For a real timing-phobic, sit the child with his back to a wall clock with a second hand.

Frame the first word in the line with the cursor, and then say 'go'. Move the cursor as fast as the pupil can read. Record the time on the sheet and tick the line off if the pupil reads every word within 10 seconds. The usual rules apply—if the child makes a mistake, you can move the cursor back and let him have another go but you cannot tick the line if you give him any help. Model and practise any word he gets stuck on and re-time that line the next day.

Unless the pupil is extremely slow, he will want to try for bonus points. You can award one bonus point if the pupil reads the line in 8 seconds, and two bonus points if he reads it in 6 seconds. You can motivate your pupil with stickers or rewards when he gets enough bonus points. If the pupil wants to have another go at a line to win a bonus point, he must wait until the following day.

Story:

The story is intended as an entertainment, so if the pupil wants to control the cursor, he may. (This is *never* allowed on any other page.) There is no tick-box for this exercise but if the pupil struggles with a sentence he should be encouraged to read it again. It may be a good idea to read the story twice to improve fluency. Model any words on which the pupil gets stuck.

FLUENCY READING

☐ Pass: 10 sec.   ☆ Bonus: 8 sec.   ⭐ Double Bonus: 6 sec.

might	boy	hoard	ledge	☐ ☆ ⭐
dock	edge	girl	beyond	☐ ☆ ⭐
shell	goth	cage	coke	☐ ☆ ⭐
fib	pence	bright	carp	☐ ☆ ⭐
lucky	skirt	cox	disarm	☐ ☆ ⭐
latch	jointed	fright	ruck	☐ ☆ ⭐
sigh	nice	tort	unhappy	☐ ☆ ⭐
turn	lash	chuck	fringe	☐ ☆ ⭐
stitch	blushes	fid	road	☐ ☆ ⭐
then	place	reload	prince	☐ ☆ ⭐
grudge	seed	queer	scotch	☐ ☆ ⭐
nosh	witch	burn	fern	☐ ☆ ⭐
extend	bird	bike	berg	☐ ☆ ⭐

The Eye of the Storm.

Mark left the bridge of Maud's rusty old trawler and went down below to help Sue shovel coal. Nate the first mate looked out over the rail. "The rocky shore of Bangalore is only a mile away," he said. "We must call for help." Neal the real seal said, "We cannot call for help because the wireless won't work. It is just like everything else on this old tub."

Maud gripped the wheel as she steered the old trawler into the huge waves. "You must shoot up a red flare and maybe someone will help us. It's all right for you two. Neal is a seal, and seals can swim. Nate can at least doggy-paddle." As she spoke, the rocky shore of Bangalore crept closer and closer.

Down below, Mark found Sue the gruesome stoker. She was shovelling coal so fast that it was just a black blur going on to the fire. Steam rose from her beefy arms, and she was soaked to the skin. "Grab a shovel, Mark my lad, and give us a hand. If we can't get some more steam out of these boilers, we will not live to see the sun rise tomorrow. Shovel for your life!"

Mark was scared and he had still had no lunch, but he picked up a shovel and gave it all he was worth. The fire grew a little hotter, and the screw turned a little faster. Mark was so tired he could hardly see, but he kept on shovelling. He started to feel a little dizzy, and Sue the gruesome stoker slapped his cheeks to keep him awake. "Here my lad, have a sip of sweet tea. It will make you strong."

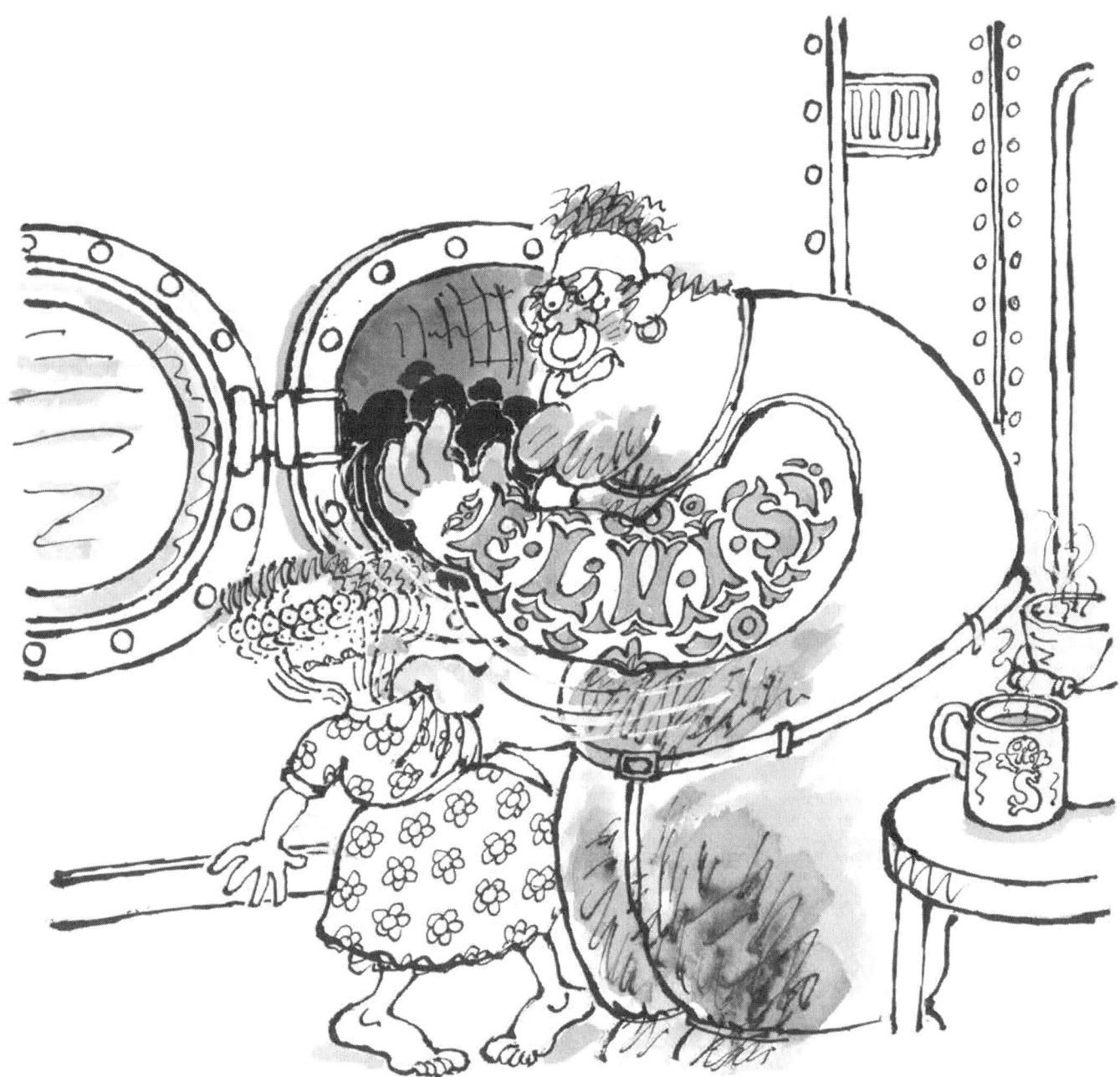

Mark drank the sweet tea, and he felt a little better. He felt a lot better because Sue knew that he was really a boy. They shovelled for ages. There was a speaking tube from the bridge, and they could hear the excited voices. Then Nate the first mate shouted down, "We are almost on the rocks! Give it all you can!" Nate was an old sea dog, but they could tell he was scared. At last, Mark passed out. He really did need his lunch.

When he woke up, Sue the gruesome stoker was washing him with cold water. The trawler was still rolling, but the wind was gone. "Well, my lad, we are in the eye of the storm. For a little while, we can rest. And when we come out of the eye of the storm, the wind will be coming from the other way. So we just might live to see another day."

Do you think Mark cared how dirty his dress was?

-le, cure, pure, sure

Always use the cursor!

| sure | pure | cure | lure | insure | assure | ☐ |

| single | gargle | puddle | needle | purple | uncle | ☐ |

| handle | kettle | Bible | table | maple | bubble | ☐ |

Are you sure you didn't step in a single puddle? ☐

If you gargle salt water, it will cure your sore throat. ☐

Bert's candles are made from pure beeswax. ☐

Gail will mend your purple jumper if you find a needle. ☐

Carl's uncle went fishing for trout with his new lure. ☐

You must pick up the kettle by the handle. ☐

The Bible is the book in the middle of the maple table. ☐

| rifle | uncle | bottle | little | able | riddle | ☐ |

| puzzle | cattle | rustle | idle | simple | ankle | ☐ |

Are you sure your uncle took his new rifle? ☐

Give the little baby his bottle and he will stop crying. ☐

Joan is able to solve hard puzzles and riddles. ☐

If you rustle cattle, you will end up in prison. ☐

Jake is just idle, pure and simple. ☐

A plaster cast is the cure for a broken ankle. ☐

DECODING ⚡ POWER ⚡ PAGE

Remember to practise the flashcards every day.

aware	admire	care	blare	☐
angle	pure	uncle	fiddle	☐
scrawny	brightest	unscrew	caught	☐
handle	scramble	cure	middle	☐
hewn	newt	shrew	knew	☐
fare	dire	scare	shire	☐
cure	riddle	little	table	☐
spite	quote	rice	ate	☐
voices	strutting	swiftly	squirting	☐
turtle	stumble	pickle	lure	☐
dare	fire	square	wire	☐
flawless	haunted	redraw	taught	☐
purple	insure	single	puzzle	☐
newest	duelling	Tuesday	value	☐
injure	buckle	tangle	Bible	☐
hire	fire	flare	pare	☐
candle	stable	idle	pure	☐
strip	scratch	shrunken	thrush	☐

Wordbuilder

If your pupil makes a mistake, back up the cursor and sound out the word.

wrong	wrongful	wrongfully	☐
cuse	accuse	accused	☐
dress	address	addressed	☐
hitch	hitched	unhitched	☐
judge	judged	misjudged	☐

Maud was wrongfully accused of stealing an apple. ☐

Are you sure that letter is addressed to my uncle? ☐

Paul unhitched the mare and put her in the stable. ☐

Spike was sent off because he misjudged his tackle. ☐

coil	coiled	recoiled	☐
fuse	refuse	refused	☐
noise	noiseless	noiselessly	☐
agree	agreement	disagreement	☐
peace	peaceful	peacefully	☐

The rifle recoiled when it was fired. ☐

The idle boy refused to go to school. ☐

Mark crept up on us noiselessly. ☐

They were able to settle their disagreement peacefully. ☐

> dead head bread read early learn war warn

You will have to learn how to make a fire if you want to get ___ .

      work   warm   wire

If your turtle hasn't moved for a year, it must be ___ .

      idle   tired   dead

We have only one loaf of bread, so we will have to ___ it.

      scare   share   sure

Be careful with that candle, it might cause a ___ .

      fiddle   fight   fire

My uncle got shot in the ___ in the last war.

      ample   ankle   axle

If you have read the book, just leave it on the ___ .

      pure   tire   table

If your dog likes to ___, it will need a muzzle.

      bike   bite   bare

I hurt my ___ when I fell off my skateboard.

      hare   hire   head

FLUENCY READING

☐ Pass: 10 sec. ☆ Bonus: 8 sec. ★ Double Bonus: 6 sec.

curl	quack	jar	budge	☐ ☆ ★
painful	barge	belay	lag	☐ ☆ ★
fir	thigh	goat	falling	☐ ☆ ★
sludge	verb	slight	saw	☐ ☆ ★
snatch	lawn	queen	join	☐ ☆ ★
beside	launch	spice	flock	☐ ☆ ★
heel	coat	cos	law	☐ ☆ ★
smudge	maul	nurse	York	☐ ☆ ★
passes	sauce	witch	quill	☐ ☆ ★
Paul	moth	fork	dredge	☐ ☆ ★
fraud	coil	drawn	bash	☐ ☆ ★
first	tuck	pause	bight	☐ ☆ ★
rid	flaw	boil	shocking	☐ ☆ ★

> giant

Amanda, the Giant Panda

Sue the gruesome stoker mopped the sweat from her face with an oily rag. Once the creaking trawler had come out of the eye of the storm, the wind had changed. It swept them out to sea again, away from the rocky shore of Bangalore. For the time being, they were safe, and Sue let Mark go to sleep on a pile of oily rags. The storm blew out by the time Mark woke up.

Mark's arms were so sore that he could hardly hold the mug of strong, sweet tea that Sue gave him. Mark was starved. He said, "Look, this story has gone too far. If I don't get my lunch now, I will leave this story. I am fed up to my back teeth with being hungry. This has gone beyond a joke."

Sue looked at Mark sadly. She said, "Well, this story wouldn't be the same without you. It looks like we will have to feed you." So Sue went to the speaking tube and shouted up to the bridge, "Now that Mark has saved your skins, the least you can do is give him some lunch!" Mark could hear some noise coming from the speaking tube, and at last he could hear Maud say, "Are you sure he can have lunch? I think it might be against the rules."

Then Sue let off steam. It came out of her nose and mouth, and it came out of her left ear. It even came out of her right ear. She flexed her beefy arms, and sweat rolled down her cheeks. Her blue tattoo turned bright red. She yelled up to the bridge, "This little boy saved your life! Unless he gets his

lunch right now, I will come up on the bridge and feed you all to the sharks!"

Up on the bridge, they were all just as scared of Sue the gruesome stoker as they had been scared of the storm. Neal the real seal flapped his flippers and said, "What can we give him? I have eaten all of the small prawns. There are none left." Nate the first mate said, "Well, Mark is not a seal, and I should think he would be just as happy with an apple sauce pizza and some cream cakes. We must go and fetch him from the boiler room, and take him to the mess decks. Amanda the giant panda can give him his lunch." So Nate the first mate grabbed a new pipe and stuffed it with shag. He struck a match and puffed until the shag was on fire. He blew a huge cloud of smoke out of his ears. Who would dare to face Sue?

Do you think that Mark will get his lunch at last?

Mastery Test

Any pupil who does not pass this test must go back to page 9. This is very important—a child who is struggling will not be learning. Contrary to what you would think, most children would rather go back than carry on getting things wrong. If the pupil needs to go back, use a different coloured pencil for ticking the boxes.

Use the cursor as you would on a Fluency Reading page.

Timed reading: 'Pass' mark is 15 seconds per line.

sure	square	fire	wrongfully	☐
hire	misjudged	little	care	☐
supermarket	admire	single	table	☐
simple	repayable	puzzle	discount	☐

Reading accuracy: Pass mark is one mistake.
Do not prompt. You may allow the pupil to self correct, but you cannot say anything except "Try again".

I am sure my uncle took the last bottle of coke. ☐

You must be careful with candles or you might start a fire. ☐

Herb broke his ankle while trying to jump over the puddle. ☐

If you gargle with salt water, it will cure your sore throat. ☐

-are, -ire: Longer words

If a pupil makes a mistake, back up the cursor and then sound out the word.

spitfire	vampire	campfire	ensnare	inspire	☐
entire	aspire	warfare	crossfire	bonfire	☐
beware	perspire	declare	require	quagmire	☐
bonfire	desire	square	empire	hardware	☐

My grandad flew a Spitfire in the Second World War. ☐

We sat around the campfire and talked about vampires. ☐

Can Clive get some wire fence at the hardware store? ☐

A good teacher can inspire you to work a lot harder. ☐

I don't think Bruce's trainers can compare with mine. ☐

Beware of the burning embers from the bonfire! ☐

retire	umpire	backfire	conspire	nightmare	☐
welfare	admire	expire	prepare	childcare	☐
enquire	software	gunfire	wildfire	ensnare	☐

Will we learn about childcare at high school? ☐

Steve had a nightmare about the sound of gunfire. ☐

I really admire Jean's new flares. ☐

When will our parking permit expire? ☐

James jumped a mile when he heard Roy's car backfire. ☐

You will be required to declare your welfare payments. ☐

DECODING POWER PAGE

Some of these words are unusual but they are all real words.

dribble	fable	cure	rifle	☐
retire	prepare	umpire	nightmare	☐
splotch	kitchen	flight	ledge	☐
misfire	software	vampire	compare	☐
disagree	excuse	splutter	baleful	☐
lure	maple	bangle	squiggle	☐
welfare	gunfire	beware	require	☐
clew	strew	flue	withdrew	☐
madness	preserve	exploit	disable	☐
declare	spitfire	hardware	satire	☐
turtle	trifle	sure	apple	☐
spate	astute	mope	incline	☐
warfare	enquire	childcare	backfire	☐
fraught	haunches	audible	saunter	☐
entire	software	airfare	haywire	☐
sable	pure	tickle	needle	☐
unaware	aspire	crossfire	firmware	☐
palace	surge	irksome	since	☐

Wordbuilder

Do not award ticks for a 'good try'—your pupil will pay for it later!

| feat | defeat | defeated | undefeated | ☐ |

| treat | treated | retreated | | ☐ |

| may | dismay | dismayed | undismayed | ☐ |

| joy | enjoy | enjoying | | ☐ |

| tire | retire | retirement | | ☐ |

The defeated army retreated to the castle. ☐

Clair was dismayed when she found the dead rat. ☐

My grandad is really enjoying his retirement. ☐

| *clare* | declare | declared | | ☐ |

| tire | entire | entirely | | ☐ |

| pare | prepare | prepared | | ☐ |

| *quire* | require | requirement | requirements | ☐ |

| *pute* | compute | computer | | ☐ |

Kent declared at two hundred for three. ☐

I am not entirely sure that is the right job for Steve. ☐

Dawn prepared a lovely packed lunch for our hike. ☐

Paul didn't meet the requirements for that school. ☐

This new computer software is useless. ☐

> pretty, does, goes, trouble, double, people, idea, poor

Luke goes to a lot of trouble to _____ a nice lunch.

    prepare   compare   admire

I had no _____ that Jean was so poor.

    fuel   idea   fault

How many years until your dad _____?

    stares   paddles   retires

Does Peter know how many _____ will require help?

    newts   people   prawns

I am pretty sure that James made a fair _____.

    tackle   tickle   triple

If you work hard you can _____ your cash.

    double   trouble   bubble

When Charles goes to school, he takes an _____ for his teacher.

    nettle   apple   beetle

Where does Joy get all of her bright _____?

    idles   ideas   pickles

FLUENCY READING

☐ Pass: 10 sec.   ☆ Bonus: 8 sec.   ★ Double Bonus: 6 sec.

plaice	quilting	drawl	thug	☐ ☆ ★
North	dodge	rain	yawn	☐ ☆ ★
flight	perch	draw	art	☐ ☆ ★
export	claw	toy	singe	☐ ☆ ★
trike	god	thaw	beet	☐ ☆ ★
retch	perk	brawn	sir	☐ ☆ ★
pain	larch	thick	sister	☐ ☆ ★
raw	nigh	torch	darn	☐ ☆ ★
haul	quit	chill	hitch	☐ ☆ ★
cause	fault	thorn	cake	☐ ☆ ★
lee	church	vault	horse	☐ ☆ ★
cadge	ashes	taut	wit	☐ ☆ ★
path	rage	stressful	pail	☐ ☆ ★

On the Mess Decks

Neal the real seal and Nate the first mate tossed a coin to see who would have to go down to the boiler room and fetch Mark up to the mess decks. They were both scared of Sue, the gruesome stoker. Neal flipped a coin (for seals have good flippers), and Nate called "Heads!". But the coin landed on Neal's tail. So Nate said, "Well, it looks like I am in dire trouble. Whoever goes below will have to face Sue, the gruesome stoker. Compared to that, walking into a bonfire would be a real treat." With a huge puff on his pipe, he left the bridge and went down to the boiler room.

35

When Sue the gruesome stoker saw Nate, she said "Bad dog! go lay down!" Nate curled his tail between his legs and slunk off to the pile of oily rags. Then he rolled over on his back and waved his legs around in the air. Sue roared with mirth. "Ha! Ho! you silly old sea-dog. You had better take Mark up to the mess decks quickly, or you will really get into trouble. Now scram!"

Sue chased Nate out of the boiler room with a coal shovel. Mark went up the ladder after him, for he was truly starved and he did not want to miss his lunch, not even if it was applesauce pizza. They went all over the rusty trawler until at last they found the mess decks. Amanda the giant panda was mopping the tables with a filthy old mop. She was huge. Even compared to Sue the gruesome stoker, she was big. She asked Nate, "Who is this little girl in the dirty dress? What is she doing in my mess decks?" Nate said, "This is Mark, and he is really a boy. He saved this rusty trawler from the rocky shore of Bangalore. He went down into the boiler room to shovel coal in the middle of the storm. You have to admire him for that. Now he is hungry and he needs some lunch. Maud said that you will have to feed him."

Amanda put down her mop. "Since we are out of small prawns, all that is left is apple-sauce pizza and cream cakes. I have not got time to prepare food for everyone who wants to eat in the middle of the day." Nate said, "Well that is fine by me, but if Sue hears that you have not fed Mark the nosh that he wants, she will come after you with a shovel." Amanda grumbled and put down her mop. "Well, you had better come here then, and we will see what we can find in our fridge."

Do you think Mark will like his lunch?

Dropping the 'e'

If a pupil makes a mistake, back up the cursor and then sound out the word.

hide	hiding	take	taking	ride	ridable
shave	shaving	fine	final	spike	spiky
smile	smiling	care	caring	stone	stony

My friends are all hiding in the barn.

Are you taking all your books to school?

That old bike is no longer ridable.

My dad cut himself shaving this morning.

We went to watch the cup-final last year.

Mark is the boy with the spiky brown hair.

smoke	smoky	shine	shiny	take	taking
scare	scary	write	writing	trade	trading
use	usable	bone	bony	bride	bridal

The room got smoky when Jean lit the fire.

The rides at the fun-fair were very scary.

Maud is writing a long letter to her sister.

Mike is trading his bike for a new tape deck.

This old software is barely usable.

Do you mind him taking one of those shiny red apples?

Dropping the 'e'

Do not award ticks for a 'good try'—your pupil will pay for it later!

shine   shining   hope   hoping   style   stylish   ☐

ride   riding   use   using   slime   slimy   ☐

globe   global   fire   firing   love   lovable   ☐

You can see the headlights shining from three miles away. ☐

Dawn was hoping you would go out riding today. ☐

Jane thinks her new trainers are very stylish. ☐

Is June still using the computer? ☐

Joyce hates picking up those slimy eels. ☐

Do you think that global warming is caused by man? ☐

size   sizable   tickle   ticklish   tide   tidal   ☐

shade   shady   drive   drivable   prune   pruning   ☐

spine   spinal   joke   joking   close   closing   ☐

Luke's dog took a sizable chunk out of my ankle. ☐

Are the soles of Paul's feet ticklish?. ☐

You must be careful when you go paddling in tidal waters. ☐

When it's hot, we sit on the shady side of the garden. ☐

Spike's old white van is no longer drivable. ☐

Drew is pruning the hedge with my old clippers. ☐

DECODING ⚡ POWER ⚡ PAGE

Some of these words are unusual but they are all real words.

ensnare	aspire	hectare	quagmire	☐
smiling	shiny	taking	cared	☐
tumble	pure	rifle	able	☐
hiding	rider	shaving	final	☐
hoarding	detailed	employed	usefully	☐
outstare	wildfire	desire	stoneware	☐
spiky	scared	trading	usable	☐
sewer	jewel	rueful	argue	☐
cradle	spindle	sure	axle	☐
smoker	writing	scary	bridal	☐
empire	daycare	crossfire	conspire	☐
raging	curved	saucy	girlish	☐
bony	caring	used	ridable	☐
slaughter	fawning	assault	hawk	☐
tidal	stony	fused	hoping	☐
acquire	nightmare	perspire	campfire	☐
shining	lovable	slimy	joker	☐
bumble	dangle	pimple	lure	☐

Wordbuilder

If your pupil makes a mistake, back up the cursor and sound out the word.

drive   drivable ☐

use   using   reusing ☐

quote   quoting   misquoting ☐

sale   salable   unsalable ☐

come   become   becoming   unbecoming ☐

Max's car was not drivable after he hit our apple tree. ☐

Mum is reusing her old jars for her pickles and jams. ☐

I think Sue is misquoting the speech. ☐

The shop's goods were unsalable after the fire. ☐

On Gail, that hat is most unbecoming. ☐

store   storing   restoring ☐

fine   final   finally ☐

close   closing   disclosing ☐

plete   complete   completely ☐

tame   tamable   untamable ☐

My grandad is good at restoring old clocks. ☐

They are finally disclosing the truth about the war. ☐

Most big cats are completely untamable. ☐

> food, school, choose, shoot, soon, room, word, worth, work

I am afraid your teacher wants a ____ with your mum.

    worm   word   worth

I like to get up at dawn and watch the ____ rising.

    moon   soon   sun

Spading over this ____ soil is hard work.

    stony   smoky   scary

Does Vern want to go ____ if the lake freezes over?

    smoking   sailing   skating

Which shooting school did your uncle ____?

    choose   choice   chance

If I want to get any work done, I have to go up to my ____.

    food   root   room

If you join the Air Force, you might fly all over the ____.

    word   world   worm

Does your school make you use joined-up ____?

    righting   writing   biting

FLUENCY READING

☐ Pass: 10 sec.　☆ Bonus: 8 sec.　⭐ Double Bonus: 6 sec.

haunch	Wight	chock	jaunt	☐ ☆ ⭐
forge	botch	jaw	nib	☐ ☆ ⭐
snitch	craw	sigh	Turk	☐ ☆ ⭐
quiz	pack	distort	patch	☐ ☆ ⭐
trawl	cake	much	glitch	☐ ☆ ⭐
sawn	clutch	slurp	shin	☐ ☆ ⭐
pledge	faun	nigh	flaunt	☐ ☆ ⭐
bob	midge	slice	restock	☐ ☆ ⭐
thigh	wack	paw	fluke	☐ ☆ ⭐
fight	yaw	torn	park	☐ ☆ ⭐
trudge	farce	high	saucer	☐ ☆ ⭐
ten	drudge	prawn	crutch	☐ ☆ ⭐
cringe	porch	deck	sledge	☐ ☆ ⭐

The Fridge

Amanda the giant panda took Mark over to the fridge. It was a very big fridge, because Amanda had to feed the entire crew of the trawler. She opened the door, and they walked in. Mark's nose was assaulted by many strange smells. "Well, let us see what we can feed you. We have lots of left-overs, perhaps we can find something you might like. Here is some crab's feet with blue cheese sauce. If you don't fancy that, maybe you would like some pot noodles with liver and custard. And for a sweet, we still have some bacon-and-egg ice cream."

Now Mark was starved. He wanted food very, very badly. He was so weak that he could hardly stand up. He felt so light-headed that he might faint at any time. But he did not think he could bring himself to eat some pot noodles with liver and custard. Now he knew why Neal the real seal stuck with the small prawns. "What else do you have?" he asked. Amanda took him further back into the fridge. It looked like no one had been back that far for years. Gobs of green goo clung to the dishes, and long strings of slime hung from the shelves. "Ah, here is the clams with peanut butter and chives. I have been looking for that for ages. It is really nice! Or maybe you would care for frog fingers with lard and leek leaves. It is all very yummy."

At this point Mark really did faint. "Oh dear," Amanda said. "Sue the gruesome stoker will not be too happy about this. I had better make sure that she does not find out." So Amanda picked Mark up and hauled him out of the fridge. She laid him out on a table. She slapped his face and forced his eyes open. Nothing helped. Mark was out cold. He had gone so long without food that he was very weak. The dreadful smell in Amanda's fridge was the last straw. Amanda became very frightened. What could she do?

While Amanda was running around in a panic, Mark was having a dream. He was back at the pub on the river, and Dawn came up to him and said, "This is your lucky day. You will not have to eat hedgehog crisps because I have saved a lovely treat for you! You will really like our snails in garlic butter." Dawn put down a tray in front of Mark, and he saw lots of snails swimming around in the melted garlic butter. But at one end of the tray, there was a snail sitting on a chair. Someone had painted "for sale" on his shell in green paint. Mark shouted, "Why it's Froid! What are you doing here?"

Froid said, "I have got a job as a life-guard. I have to save anyone who is drowning in garlic butter. But us snails are fine in garlic butter, so I don't have much to do."

Mark said, "I think Dawn expects me to eat you. I couldn't eat an old mate." Froid said, "Don't worry. Only frogs eat snails." With this, Froid picked up a guitar and started to sing a song.

How much do you think Froid would fetch on eBay?

Mastery Test

Any pupil who does not pass this test must go back to page 30. This is very important—a child who is struggling will not be learning. Contrary to what you would think, most children would rather go back than carry on getting things wrong. If the pupil needs to go back, use a different coloured pencil for ticking the boxes.

Use the cursor as you would on a Fluency Reading page.

Timed reading: 'Pass' mark is 15 seconds per line.

require	enjoyed	hiding	lovable	☐
joking	welfare	entire	smoky	☐
taking	shiny	bonfire	computer	☐
completely	caring	writing	declare	☐

Reading accuracy: Pass mark is one mistake.
Do not prompt. You may allow the pupil to self correct, but you cannot say anything except "Try again".

Bruce could get some steel wire at the hardware store. ☐

Jane is taking our car because hers in no longer drivable. ☐

Do you wake up when you have a nightmare? ☐

Are you reusing these jars for making your pickles? ☐

-ion

Always use the cursor!

quest   question   questionable ☐

state   station   stationary ☐

rel   relate   relation   relations ☐

My little sister is always asking questions. ☐

How far is it to the bus station? ☐

Of all my relations, I like Uncle Mike the best. ☐

vac   vacate   vacation ☐

rect   direct   direction   directions ☐

oper   operate   operation ☐

Last summer, we went to Spain for our vacation. ☐

If you get lost, just stop and ask for directions. ☐

My gran just had an operation on her hip. ☐

port   portion   portions ☐

fect   infect   infection ☐

fuse   confuse   confusion ☐

Could I have a large portion of chips, please? ☐

The robber got away in all the confusion. ☐

You should keep that cut clean or you might get an infection. ☐

Wordbuilder

If your pupil makes a mistake, back up the cursor and sound out the word.

mit   *imit*   imitate   imitation   ☐

don   donate   donation   ☐

spect   inspect   inspection   ☐

I want a real sheepskin coat, not one of those cheap imitations.   ☐

My mum always gives a donation to a good cause.   ☐

Please have your boarding passes ready for inspection.   ☐

cor   decor   decorate   decoration   ☐

viol   violate   violation   violations   ☐

probe   probate   probation   ☐

Can I paint some decorations on my wall?   ☐

Why does your dad get so many parking violations?   ☐

The robber was lucky that the judge only gave him probation.   ☐

pollute   pollution   ☐

tense   tension   extension   ☐

ject   object   objection   objections   ☐

We spend a lot of time at school studying pollution.   ☐

I was late with my work, but my teacher gave me an extension.   ☐

I am going to have a bath, if you don't have any objections. ☐

49

DECODING ~ POWER ~ PAGE

Some of these words are unusual but they are all real words..

taping	spinal	tradable	sized	☐
question	action	portion	mention	☐
esquire	shareware	inspire	beware	☐
mission	fashion	session	passion	☐
ladle	puddle	shuffle	cure	☐
finest	becoming	quotable	rider	☐
pension	tension	mansion	version	☐
bluest	dewy	stewing	brewer	☐
compare	vampire	bonfire	welfare	☐
station	nation	operation	relation	☐
smoking	shady	ripest	drivable	☐
mawkish	gauzy	applauding	saunter	☐
confusion	pollution	probation	imitation	☐
ankle	bugle	lure	hustle	☐
donation	imitation	violation	decoration	☐
tidy	hating	livable	stolen	☐
direction	infection	inspection	injection	☐
expire	warfare	admire	declare	☐

> ready, instead, heavy, healthy, heard, search, warning

Did James give a _____ to the Red Cross?

    infection   donation   station

You can't see many stars at night because of the ____ pollution.

    heard   light   noise

Spike got probation _____ of going to prison.

    instead   inside   insight

Be sure you are _____ to go when you hear the warning.

    really   read   ready

If you want to stay healthy, you must avoid getting _____.

    infections   injections   directions

Paul had to get an _____ ladder to reach the roof.

    imitation   operation   extension

Have you _____ about all the trouble at school?

    heard   held   herb

Jane had to _____ all over the house to find her book.

    stretch   stitch   search

FLUENCY READING

☐ Pass: 10 sec.   ☆ Bonus: 8 sec.   ★ Double Bonus: 6 sec.

taunt	poach	spike	spawn	☐ ☆ ★
blight	swirl	weep	boy	☐ ☆ ★
crotch	goth	Dutch	gawk	☐ ☆ ★
haunt	match	tort	road	☐ ☆ ★
smirk	unspoilt	blotch	Maud	☐ ☆ ★
nosh	woke	wedge	sketch	☐ ☆ ★
made	berg	brawl	these	☐ ☆ ★
light	age	goat	chick	☐ ☆ ★
tube	fawn	shine	batch	☐ ☆ ★
shim	failed	cube	sludge	☐ ☆ ★
hide	coat	vaunt	wide	☐ ☆ ★
taut	mole	hers	quill	☐ ☆ ★
grudge	lance	wise	maul	☐ ☆ ★

Scary Mary the Kitchen Maid.

While Mark was laid out on the table dreaming about Froid and his guitar, Amanda the giant panda was running around in a panic. Scary Mary the kitchen maid came down from the bridge with a tray full of dirty tea mugs and she said, "What is that dirty little girl doing on my table? Now I will have to wash it again. I have already had one health warning this week."

Just then, Sue the gruesome stoker came storming in, waving a dirty coal shovel in the air. "What have you done to my Mark?" she boomed. "He saved your life, and now you have killed him with your cooking." With this, she swung the shovel at Amanda, and gave her two black eyes. Or she would have done, except that pandas already have black eyes.

Amanda dived under the table, but she was so big that the table tipped over, and Mark rolled off and fell to the filthy deck. Sue roared out, "Get down in the boiler room and shovel coal, you useless panda! I will look after Mark." Amanda darted away, and Scary Mary started to run too, hoping that she could get away in all the confusion. But Sue caught her by the scruff of her neck. "You will stay here, you vampire. You will mop and scrub until the mess decks are spotless. And you will wash Mark's dress."

Scary Mary wiped her nose on her sleeve and snivelled, but she did as she was told. Sue made her wash and dry a table, and she made her get a clean blanket to keep Mark warm. Then Sue put on the kettle and made a cup of tea, using three teabags for herself and one for Mark. "I guess my tea might be a little too strong for the young lad," she said.

But Mark did not wake up just yet. He was nice and warm in his soft blanket. He dreamed that he was riding Hank, the hunch-backed horse. "I hate to say this," Mark said, "but the train was faster. And the seats were more comfortable, too." Hank said, "When we see Floyd the faultless fish, we can ask him for directions to the train station." In his dream, Mark was eating fish and chips, which tasted ever so good. "Oh dear," he said, "I hope I haven't just eaten him."

Do you think Mary is scary?

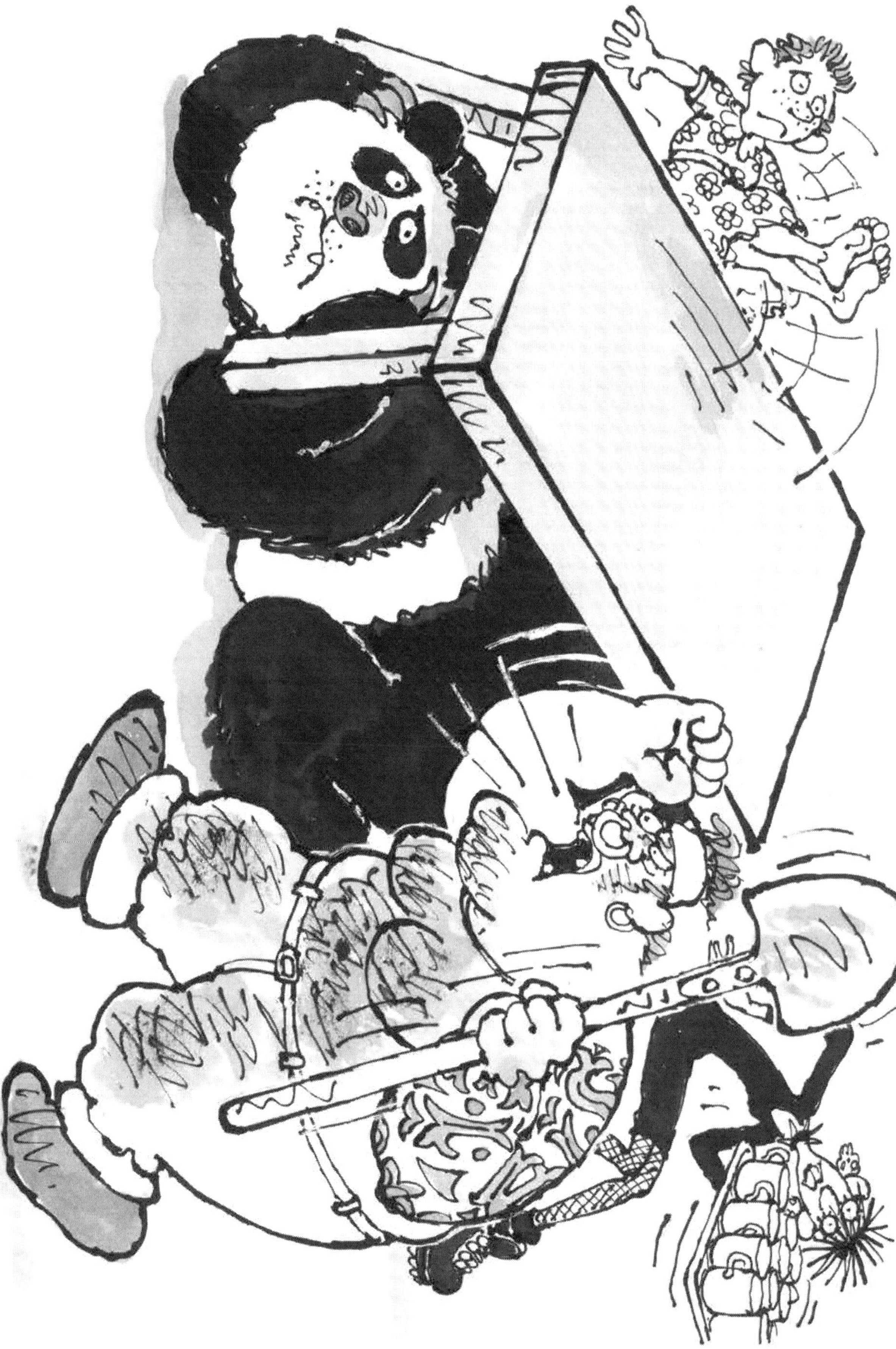

Dropping the 'e'

If a pupil makes a mistake, back up the cursor and then sound out the word.

hide   hiding   scare   scary   bride   bridal   ☐

come   coming   fire   firing   ride   ridable   ☐

fine   final   wipe   wiping   dine   dining   ☐

Jess is hiding behind the chair because the film is so scary. ☐

Eve wore her gran's bridal dress to her wedding. ☐

The shooters are coming back when they finish firing their rifles. ☐

Clive's old bike is barely ridable. ☐

Is Steve going to watch the cup final with us? ☐

dare   daring   scare   scaring   spike   spiky   ☐

drive   driving   shine   shiny   smoke   smoky   ☐

tube   tubing   like   likable   use   using   ☐

June is wiping the crumbs off the dining room table. ☐

Joyce is always daring me to jump off the roof. ☐

Pete got into trouble for scaring those poor old people. ☐

Mark is the boy with the spiky brown hair. ☐

The dining room gets pretty smoky when Dad is cooking. ☐

Uncle Max replaced the leaky pipes with some new copper tubing. ☐

DECODING ~ POWER ~ PAGE

Do not award ticks for a 'good try'—your pupil will pay for it later!

infection	rejection	nation	question	☐
using	lazy	latest	joking	☐
prepare	haywire	software	bonfire	☐
closing	tamable	riding	wider	☐
cable	puzzle	lure	nestle	☐
imitation	inspection	extension	objection	☐
bridal	shiny	loved	pruning	☐
merger	surfboard	graceless	handsome	☐
witchcraft	chainmail	poacher	quirky	☐
daring	noting	baby	stolen	☐
pollution	station	direction	confusion	☐
frightful	crutches	edgy	tightrope	☐
salable	tubing	crazy	scared	☐
tingle	noble	cure	beetle	☐
firing	likable	smoky	final	☐
tension	relation	operation	portion	☐
hectare	umpire	hardware	esquire	☐
spiky	wiping	skated	dining	☐

Wordbuilder

Always use the cursor!

add   addition   additional   ☐

tire   retire   retiring   ☐

ject object   objection   objections ☐

We had to hire additional workers for the heavy jobs. ☐

I heard that my uncle James is retiring in June. ☐

If you have no objections, we will go to the beach instead. ☐

miss   mission   permission   ☐

fine   final   finalist   finalists   ☐

take   mistake   mistakable unmistakable ☐

Does Maud have permission to trawl for prawns? ☐

The finalists on Big Brother are all twits. ☐

Ruth is unmistakable with her green hair. ☐

spire   inspire   inspiring   uninspiring ☐

flect reflect   reflection   ☐

fashion fashionable unfashionable ☐

Our new headmaster gave an inspiring talk last week. ☐

Can you see your reflection in the glass? ☐

Vern is too big to care if his trainers are unfashionable. ☐

58

> guess, guest, guitar, guard, guide, guilty, sign

We just passed a ____ saying the road is closed ahead.

    sing   sign   singe

Uncle Bert will be staying in the _____ room.

    guess   guest   guilty

I can't play the _____ because all the strings are broken.

    guide   guitar   guess

The guards took the _____ man back to the jail.

    healthy   early   guilty

Your bright ____ always seem to get us in trouble.

    itches   inches   ideas

Peter got a job as a life _____ at the swimming pool.

    guard   guide   guitar

You must ____ your name here if you want to go skating.

    sign   slime   size

We are sure to get lost if you can't find the street ____.

    guide   global   sweeper

FLUENCY READING

☐ Pass: 10 sec.   ☆ Bonus: 8 sec.   ★ Double Bonus: 6 sec.

join	tale	pledge	bite	☐ ☆ ★
gormless	light	lard	hack	☐ ☆ ★
home	crawl	hope	gaunt	☐ ☆ ★
boil	safe	notch	curb	☐ ☆ ★
tame	quell	pawn	stone	☐ ☆ ★
might	oak	weed	day	☐ ☆ ★
lone	itch	June	haul	☐ ☆ ★
shock	lane	thaw	wipe	☐ ☆ ★
Wight	perch	twirl	note	☐ ☆ ★
auk	mule	pain	beet	☐ ☆ ★
fetch	vainly	tape	date	☐ ☆ ★
perk	plunge	witch	urn	☐ ☆ ★
jaw	toy	frailest	same	☐ ☆ ★

| pirate |

Lunch At Last?

Mark was still dreaming. He was riding Hank the hunch-backed horse, and he was eating fish and chips. Then he started to wake up, because he really did smell fish and chips. "About time you stirred yourself," said Sue the gruesome stoker. "I was starting to worry about you. I sent Scary Mary out for some fish and chips, because there's nothing fit to eat in Amanda's kitchen. Here's a nice big portion of skate and chips for you."

Mark was pretty sure that Floyd wasn't a skate, and he was starving. He had gone for thirty-three pages without a bite to eat, and it didn't seem possible that they would let him have his lunch at last. Mark sat up and reached for his portion of skate and chips—could it really be for real? Or was it just an imitation? Was he still dreaming?

The bag of chips felt nice and warm in his hands. But just as he reached for his first chip, he heard the crack of gunfire. The steel deck above his head rang out with the crash of heavy boots. "Why, it must be Jolly Roger the pirate, drunk again," said Sue. "You just stay here and enjoy your chips while I go and sort him out." Sue got up and stomped off in the direction of the noise.

Mark ran after her, but he tripped over Scary Mary, who was trying to hide under a table. Mark sprawled out on his face, and his fish and chips spilled out on the grimy deck. He was so hungry that he was tempted to eat them anyway. He had eaten two chips and one bite of skate, and he was more hungry than ever. But the deck smelled of rotten cheese and dirty socks, with a hint of moist dog. It smelled so bad that Mark almost threw up, so he left his lunch where it had landed.

When Mark got up, his dress was dirty again. He was fed up with being a girl, and going without lunch had become a nightmare. But he had to run after Sue, because he had never seen a pirate before.

Do you think pirates are real?

Do you think Scary Mary ate Mark's chips?

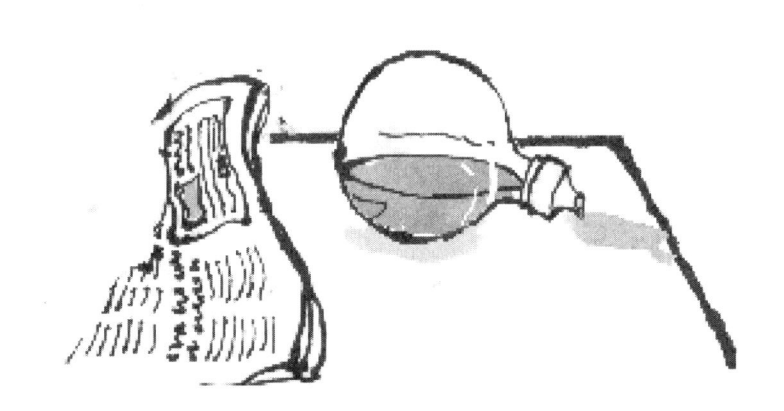

Mastery Test

Any pupil who does not pass this test must go back to page 48. This is very important—a child who is struggling will not be learning. Contrary to what you would think, most children would rather go back than carry on getting things wrong. If the pupil needs to go back, use a different coloured pencil for ticking the boxes.

Use the cursor as you would on a Fluency Reading page.

Timed reading: 'Pass' mark is 15 seconds per line.

retiring	final	direction	relation	☐
bridal	objection	admired	operation	☐
spiky	dining	inspiring	addition	☐
inspection	reaction	daring	permission	☐

Reading accuracy: Pass mark is one mistake.
Do not prompt. You may allow the pupil to self correct, but you cannot say anything except "Try again".

We must get planning permission for our new extension. ☐

Spike is unmistakable, driving his shiny purple car. ☐

Please have your boarding passes ready for inspection. ☐

Jess thinks that my bright red trainers are unfashionable. ☐

Dancing Bears

Well done!

You have completed
Level 8

You are now working on Level 9

Soft 'c'

If a pupil makes a mistake, back up the cursor and then sound out the word.

race   racer   fence   fencing   choice   choicest   ☐

slice   sliced   nice   nicest   dance   dancing   ☐

Do boy racers smash up their cars very often? ☐

My mum sent me out to get a sliced loaf of white bread. ☐

Would you like to come dancing with us? ☐

Last summer Martin painted all the fencing brown. ☐

city   circle   cent   centre   certain   cider   ☐

I think this is the nicest part of the city. ☐

The boys were racing around in a circle. ☐

In the USA, a dime is worth ten cents. ☐

I am certain that the castle is in the city centre. ☐

Little boys and girls should never drink strong cider. ☐

cell   cellar   circus   Cecil   cinema   cigar   ☐

The judge put the bank-robber in a jail cell. ☐

Joan's house has a very damp cellar. ☐

Bruce saw a tight-rope walker at the circus. ☐

My uncle Cecil likes to smoke a cigar after dinner. ☐

Would you like to go to the cinema tonight? ☐

DECODING ⚡ POWER ⚡ PAGE

Do not award ticks for a 'good try'—your pupil will pay for it later!

quaking	driver	ridable	spoken	☐
cider	sliced	nicer	cent	☐
addition	aversion	division	reaction	☐
cell	city	racer	fencing	☐
ensnare	retire	shareware	inspire	☐
brutal	gazed	fluky	swiping	☐
circle	dancing	centre	fencing	☐
fickle	jungle	stifle	cure	☐
vacation	vision	question	position	☐
Cecil	facing	circus	nicest	☐
taken	racing	gravy	scored	☐
jaunt	threw	awkward	Tuesday	☐
choicest	cinema	cigar	fencing	☐
empire	stare	quagmire	daycare	☐
tracing	cellar	certain	placed	☐
tamer	shady	lining	notable	☐
cider	city	centre	circus	☐
rejection	portion	tension	imitation	☐

Wordbuilder

If your pupil makes a mistake, back up the cursor and sound out the word.

cite   excite   excited   unexcited   ☐

cent   percent   percentage   ☐

cide   decide   decided   undecided   ☐

Martha was very excited about our new puppy.   ☐

We had to pay a tax of ten percent.   ☐

Please tell me what you have decided to do.   ☐

ceed   succeed   succeeding   ☐

ceive   receive   received   ☐

cept   except   exception   exceptions   ☐

You must try harder if you do not succeed at first.   ☐

I sent Dawn a letter but she never received it.   ☐

I am sorry, but we can't make any exceptions to the rules.   ☐

cel   excel   excellent   excellently   ☐

cess   success   successful   successfully   ☐

cent   recent   recently   ☐

Luke got excellent grades at school last term.   ☐

If you work hard, you will certainly be successful.   ☐

The circus was in the city very recently.   ☐

| does, goes, trouble, people, idea, poor, door, floor |

Steve is a real ____ on the dance floor.

    startle   start   star

My Uncle Cecil goes to a lot of _____ to help poor people.

    triple   trouble   tension

Clair's ideas are always _____ .

    excellent   excited   exceptions

Does Charles know the way into the ____?

    cigar   cider   city

How many bottles of wine are in your uncle's _____?

    circle   circus   cellar

You can draw a ____ if you trace around a saucer.

    square   goat   circle

Are you certain that Sue left the back door _____?

    locked   licked   looked

How many stations can you _____ on your tuner?

    receive   succeed   decide

FLUENCY READING

☐ Pass: 10 sec. ☆ Bonus: 8 sec. ✪ Double Bonus: 6 sec.

daub	hinge	perk	pain	☐ ☆ ✪
switch	irk	Pete	paw	☐ ☆ ✪
torch	purse	life	murk	☐ ☆ ✪
dodge	darn	sage	awl	☐ ☆ ✪
reborn	side	rain	chub	☐ ☆ ✪
law	lurk	fudge	dice	☐ ☆ ✪
mail	rise	fraud	wage	☐ ☆ ✪
hole	marsh	chance	right	☐ ☆ ✪
flirt	gauze	thorn	ray	☐ ☆ ✪
porky	bone	cause	race	☐ ☆ ✪
ford	night	burp	pale	☐ ☆ ✪
bawl	say	voice	fuse	☐ ☆ ✪
birth	badge	horse	rack	☐ ☆ ✪

Jolly Roger

Mark looked regretfully at his fish and chips, which were strewn all over the grimy floor. As he got up, he had trouble peeling his hands and knees off the greasy deck. Then he heard some more gunfire, so he decided to run to the door and see what the excitement was about. He ran up the ladder to the main deck, where everyone was running around in confusion. Mark saw a man with a black patch over one eye, and he had a gun. He shouted, "Down with Maudlin Maud! Let's take over this trawler, and then we can have all the cider and beer that we want!"

Gruesome Sue the stoker stomped across the deck. "Jolly Roger, you are drunk already. Put down that gun, and you can sleep it off in the boiler room." Jolly Roger raised his gun and pointed it at Gruesome Sue. "Stop, or I will shoot! I really mean it!" he shouted. But Sue looked him square in the eye, and she kept on coming. As she got closer, Jolly Roger's hand began to shake. "I'll shoot!" he yelled. But Sue paid no attention to his brave words. She picked him up by the scruff of his neck, and she shook him until he dropped his gun.

"Jolly Roger, you have some pretty daft ideas, even when you are sober. You are always causing trouble, stirring up the crew. If I were Maud, I'd feed you to the sharks." But just then Scary Mary crept up behind Sue with a big club. She was angry because Sue had made her wash Mark's dress and get his chips. Mark yelled "Watch out!", but it was too late. Scary Mary hit Sue as hard as she could, and poor Sue fell to the deck. Mark ran up quickly, but it was too late—Sue was out cold.

Jolly Roger picked up his gun again, and shouted, "Let's make them walk the plank! That's the way pirates are supposed to do things." One of the other pirates mentioned that Sue was in no condition to walk anywhere. Another one said that no one knew for certain where to find a plank.

"Well, we have to do something with all of the bosses, or we will all go to jail. Maybe we could put them in the hold where we store our raw prawns." said Scary Mary. So Jolly Roger and the pirates rounded up Maud, Nate, Neal and the loyal crew, and herded them into the hold for raw prawns. It took six men to drag Sue to the hold. While they were doing this, Mark hid in a lifeboat. He was very frightened—without Sue to protect him, who could he trust?

Do you think Jolly Roger will find more cider?

-ion:

Always use the cursor.

mention   fraction   caution   attention ☐

dictation   reputation   education   action ☐

I forgot to mention it, but Uncle Cecil is coming for a visit. ☐

Maud learned how to add and subtract fractions at school. ☐

Blind people always cross streets with caution. ☐

If you do not pay attention, you will never learn anything. ☐

My teacher is always making me write from dictation. ☐

If you work hard, you will get a good reputation. ☐

My Uncle Cecil did not get a very good education. ☐

insulation   foundation   equation   detention ☐

position   junction   explosion   tradition ☐

You can save fuel by putting insulation in your loft. ☐

Gail learned how to solve simple equations last term. ☐

Our new teacher gave Dawn a detention for being late. ☐

I get fed up playing the same position in every game. ☐

They should put up stop signs at that road junction. ☐

The leaking gas main caused a big explosion. ☐

The workers dug the foundations for our new house. ☐

DECODING POWER PAGE

Do not award ticks for a 'good try'—your pupil will pay for it later!

circle	decide	cellar	excited	☐
objection	pollution	probation	decoration	☐
navy	shaken	tradable	scaring	☐
mention	vacation	inspection	fraction	☐
aspire	square	vampire	childcare	☐
tracing	city	certain	dancer	☐
caution	action	detention	education	☐
sliced	whitest	slimy	fatal	☐
muffle	idle	gamble	tremble	☐
coming	shaky	notable	spoken	☐
dictation	attention	reputation	tradition	☐
receive	cider	success	recent	☐
gunfire	pirate	declare	nightmare	☐
equation	junction	position	fashion	☐
likable	nosy	smoking	wiping	☐
addition	insulation	position	mission	☐
recent	except	cinema	succeed	☐
foundation	explosion	permission	reflection	☐

Wordbuilder

If your pupil makes a mistake, back up the cursor and sound out the word.

lax	relax	relaxation		☐
vise	vision*	television		☐
fend	defend	defender		☐
tent	intent	intention	intentional	☐
sense	sensate	sensation	sensational	☐

After a hard day in school, we need a little relaxation. ☐

Last night we watched football on the television. ☐

The Leeds United defender was sent off for an intentional foul. ☐

Spur's goal-keeper made a sensational save. ☐

cite	excite	excited	unexcited	☐
miss	mission	permission		☐
ject	inject	injection		☐
pair	repair	repaired		☐
verse	version	diversion		☐

The children were all excited about the new puppy. ☐

You can come with us if your mum gives you permission. ☐

Does the nurse have to give me an injection? ☐

The road was being repaired and we had to take a diversion. ☐

> ready, instead, heavy, healthy, heard, search, warning

All that heavy work will make you fit and _____ .

    heard   healthy   guilty

If Steve is not ready, we can take Charles _____ .

    insane   instead   insight

Paul will get a good price for his guitar if it is in good _____ .

    caution   condition   confusion

You can get that _____ by searching on the computer.

    information   injection   infection

Does that imported cigar have a _____ warning?

    health   heavy   guilty

Fay goes to a lot of trouble to make herself look _____ .

    poor   permission   pretty

June did not see the sign _____ that the bridge was closed.

    warning   warming   working

You must _____ your name here if you want to hire a van.

    sign   sing   sight

FLUENCY READING

☐ Pass: 10 sec. ☆ Bonus: 8 sec. ★ Double Bonus: 6 sec.

face	sauce	belong	theme	☐ ☆ ★
paid	Paul	shirt	hedge	☐ ☆ ★
bilge	arch	prune	dirt	☐ ☆ ★
pace	late	ash	way	☐ ☆ ★
fault	quote	notch	tune	☐ ☆ ★
quin	fleece	saw	time	☐ ☆ ★
aid	Bert	ate	verge	☐ ☆ ★
gauze	hate	pail	parch	☐ ☆ ★
birch	mile	trawl	pipe	☐ ☆ ★
verse	sight	quite	spurt	☐ ☆ ★
faun	oath	use	exact	☐ ☆ ★
Clive	lurch	form	eel	☐ ☆ ★
flaw	dude	lunge	rule	☐ ☆ ★

The Ventilation Shaft

Mark hid in the lifeboat until it was dark. The pirates found more cider, and they shouted and sang, and they smoked strong cigars. Late at night the last of them passed out. When Mark crawled out of the lifeboat, there were pirates sprawled all over the deck. They were all snoring. Mark almost tripped over Scary Mary, who was snoring the loudest of all.

The trawler was dead in the water. The boilers had run out of steam because there was no one to shovel coal. Mark walked up and down the deck. He found Jolly Roger slumped over a barrel of cider, with his gun stuck in his belt. Very carefully, Mark slipped the gun from his belt and crept away. He was very excited—with a gun, he could make the pirates let Sue and the crew out of the raw prawn hold. But when he checked the gun, there were no bullets left.

But did Jolly Roger know that his gun was empty? Mark knew that drunks are not too good at remembering things. Did he dare try to bluff Jolly Roger with an empty gun? Maybe it wasn't such a good idea. A small boy in a dirty dress would have a hard time facing down a crew of hard pirates. So Mark hid the gun in the lifeboat, and he went on searching the trawler.

When he got to the stern, he heard some barking. He traced the noise to a ventilation shaft that came out of the hold. Mark listened carefully, and he realised that Nate the first mate and Neal the real seal were barking at each other. He put his nose in the ventilation shaft (which smelled very strongly of raw prawns) and called out softly, "Sue? Are you there? Are you all right?"

The barking stopped. He could hear heavy footsteps down in the hold. At last, Sue called up, "Mark, my lad, I have a sore head, but I will live. You must be careful that the pirates don't find you, and you must try to get us out of here. You must find the door to this room." Sue gave Mark directions, so he would not get lost when he went below. Mark crept away—he was afraid that he would wake up a pirate, and then it would be all over for him.

Do you think that Jolly Roger will have a hangover?

Mastery Test

Any pupil who does not pass this test must go back to page 67. This is very important—a child who is struggling will not be learning. Contrary to what you would think, most children would rather go back than carry on getting things wrong. If the pupil needs to go back, use a different coloured pencil for ticking the boxes.

Use the cursor as you would on a Fluency Reading page.

Timed reading: 'Pass' mark is 15 seconds per line.

circle	percent	attention	fraction	☐
junction	certain	excited	education	☐
successful	cider	explosion	circus	☐
exception	decided	tradition	cell	☐

Reading accuracy: Pass mark is one mistake.
Do not prompt. You may allow the pupil to self correct, but you cannot say anything except "Try again".

We learned how to solve simple equations last term. ☐

You should never make exceptions to the rules. ☐

My teacher sent a note to my dad but he never received it. ☐

Are you certain that the circus is in the city? ☐

83

'y' to 'i':

If a pupil makes a mistake, back up the cursor and then sound out the word.

story	stories	daddy daddies	funny funniest	☐
party	parties	puppy puppies	hurry hurried	☐
lady	ladies	lorry lorries	marry married	☐
copy	copied	nanny nannies	heavy heaviest	☐

I have copied all the funniest stories in that book. ☐

Sue hurried home to see all the new puppies. ☐

The ladies are worried about their nannies. ☐

My Uncle Cecil knows how to drive the heaviest lorries. ☐

noise   noisy   noisiest   scare   scary   scariest ☐

Clive and Jane always give the noisiest parties. ☐

Steve always goes on the scariest rides. ☐

thief	thieves	grief	grieves	piece	niece	☐
belief	believe	relief	relieve	brief	chief	☐
field	yield	shield	priest	siege	achieve	☐

The sneaky thief stole a piece of cake. ☐

My niece was overcome with grief when thieves took her goat. ☐

I sent a brief note to the chief. ☐

A priest should always believe in God. ☐

DECODING POWER PAGE

Some of these words are unusual but they are all real words.

tidal	ridable	lazy	latest	☐
violation	extension	donation	inspection	☐
puppies	copied	stories	parties	☐
circus	icing	centre	excite	☐
field	lorries	nannies	married	☐
retiring	mistakable	latest	tribal	☐
addition	reflection	exception	station	☐
noisiest	chief	hurried	believe	☐
misfire	welfare	prepare	empire	☐
fencing	Cecil	cigar	racing	☐
thief	funniest	ladies	heaviest	☐
detention	mention	tradition	attention	☐
able	cured	bungle	dabble	☐
grief	copier	niece	scariest	☐
becoming	wisest	bony	final	☐
daddies	achieve	noisier	piece	☐
foundation	junction	fraction	education	☐
brief	relieve	funnier	shield	☐

Wordbuilder

Do not award ticks for a 'good try'—your pupil will pay for it later!

plore	explore	explorer	explorers	☐
cite	excite	exciting	unexciting	☐
cover	discover	discovery	discoveries	☐
feat	defeat	defeated	undefeated	☐

The explorers made many exciting discoveries. ☐

Our football team was undefeated last year. ☐

miss	mission	permission		☐
fect	affect	affection	affectionate	☐
civil	civilise	civilisation		☐

We cannot go if we do not get permission. ☐

Our new kitten is very affectionate. ☐

After a week in the jungle, the explorers got back to civilisation. ☐

spire	inspire	inspiring	uninspiring	☐
pare	prepare	preparing		☐
cept	recept	reception	receptionist	☐

A good teacher can be very inspiring. ☐

Peter and Maud spent three hours preparing lunch. ☐

The receptionist told us to take a seat. ☐

86

> thought, ought, bought, fought, busy, great, break

You cannot park those lorries in this field when it is ____.

    break   muddy   hurry

I believe my Uncle Cecil ____ in the Great War.

    fought   bought   copied

My niece is getting ____ by a priest in the church.

    hurried   married   believed

When do the ladies ____ for tea?

    bought   break   busy

We ought to get ____ before the chief gets back.

    busy   civil   cement

I thought the thief went off in that ____.

    infection   relation   direction

What do you hope to achieve by telling such ____?

    cigars   cellars   stories

We ____ to take a break before my Uncle Cecil finds us.

    thought   bought   ought

FLUENCY READING

☐ Pass: 10 sec. ☆ Bonus: 8 sec. ★ Double Bonus: 6 sec.

void	Maud	line	clutch	☐ ☆ ★
name	orb	ice	drawn	☐ ☆ ★
prevent	pole	nerve	boat	☐ ☆ ★
force	pawn	robe	furl	☐ ☆ ★
norm	first	rode	raw	☐ ☆ ★
sale	lath	cadge	shine	☐ ☆ ★
chirp	vaunt	loin	quiff	☐ ☆ ★
cope	band	rude	quirk	☐ ☆ ★
mesh	vault	swipe	mate	☐ ☆ ★
drawl	toad	change	draw	☐ ☆ ★
edge	sawn	leech	hock	☐ ☆ ★
retrain	slide	caught	mince	☐ ☆ ★
joy	dawn	ride	judge	☐ ☆ ★

Leif the Chief Thief

Sue's voice carried up the ventilation shaft so loudly that Mark was afraid that one of the pirates would wake up. She gave Mark directions so he could find his way to the door to the hold. Mark thought they were lucky to be locked in the hold—at least they had lots of raw prawns to eat. Mark went down a hatch, but it was pitch dark below. The lights on a ship at sea are not plugged into the mains, so when the fire in the boiler room went out, the old trawler had no power. So Mark went back up on deck to see if he could find a lighter. The pirates had all been smoking cigars, so Mark thought that they all must have lighters. Mark was not a thief, and he did not like the idea of picking pockets. But what else could he do?

Mark was not very good at picking pockets. The first pirate he came to smelled very strongly of cider, and he was snoring like a buzz saw. But Mark could not find a lighter in his pocket. The pirate started to wake up, and he mumbled a curse. Mark crept away. After a bit, he got up the nerve to try another sleeping pirate. His pockets were empty. Mark checked the pockets of five more pirates, but not one of them had a lighter. "What can I do?" he thought. " I must find the door so I can let Gruesome Sue and Maudlin Maud out of the hold. But I will achieve nothing if I get caught." Just then he heard footsteps. Slowly, they got closer and closer. In the moonlight, Mark saw a pirate with a cigar clamped in his teeth. Mark was so scared that he started shaking.

"Say pal, have you got a light?" the pirate asked. Mark was a little relieved. "No sir," he said. "I don't smoke." The pirate said, "Well, I will just have to find Leif the chief thief. He steals everyone's lighter when they are drunk, so his pockets must be full of them."

"If you don't mind, sir, I will come and help you. I like stealing lighters myself." Mark was fibbing, but he thought that was the sort of thing that a pirate would say. Soon they found Leif the chief thief. He was sleeping with his head in a pail of raw prawns, so he didn't snore much. His pockets bulged with lighters. Mark and the pirate took ten each. The pirate lit his cigar with a sigh of relief. "Care for a drink, pal?" he asked. Mark said, "It's past my bedtime and if my mum finds out that I am not in bed I will be in real trouble. Thanks anyway." With that, Mark slipped away to find the door to the hold.

Do you think that any of the lighters will work?

-ure

Always use the cursor!

picture   mixture   capture   torture   vulture   ☐

venture   moisture   puncture   furniture   nature   ☐

Charles enjoys drawing pictures with his blue pencil. ☐

You get to go on field trips if you take nature studies. ☐

Little Max got into trouble for jumping on the furniture. ☐

I was late for school because my bike tyre got a puncture. ☐

culture   fixture   pasture   future   lecture   ☐

feature   creature   texture   fracture   posture   ☐

Last year we studied French culture at school. ☐

Will your dad be able to repair the broken light fixture? ☐

All the cows are grazing on the fresh grass in the new pasture. ☐

I expect that you will not be so careless in the future. ☐

I hope our teacher doesn't give us another lecture. ☐

measure   treasure   pleasure   seizure   composure   ☐

You can use a ruler to measure your box. ☐

We searched for days, but we never found any treasure. ☐

When I get bored with my computer, I often read for pleasure. ☐

DECODING POWER PAGE

If a pupil makes a mistake, back up the cursor and then sound out the word.

certain	cell	tracing	nicest	☐
siege	belief	carried	scarier	☐
picture	mixture	texture	future	☐
violation	exception	insulation	action	☐
capture	vulture	pleasure	venture	☐
sliced	racing	cell	circus	☐
laziest	priest	puppies	yield	☐
puncture	measure	lecture	fixture	☐
crazy	wiped	hiding	likable	☐
caution	equation	intention	diversion	☐
torture	nature	creature	posture	☐
grieves	married	heavier	chief	☐
desire	beware	conspire	careful	☐
moisture	culture	pasture	treasure	☐
cinema	dancing	iced	cent	☐
furniture	fracture	pleasure	future	☐
piece	relief	nannies	copied	☐
feature	measure	posture	pasture	☐

Wordbuilder

Do not award ticks for a 'good try'—your pupil will pay for it later!

vent   advent   adventure ☐

part   depart   departure ☐

feat   feature   featuring ☐

capt   capture   recapture   recaptured ☐

Merl reads a lot of adventure stories. ☐

The departure of our flight was delayed for three hours. ☐

My Grandad has some DVDs featuring the Rolling Stones. ☐

The police recaptured the escaped prisoner. ☐

pose   expose   exposure ☐

close   disclose   disclosure ☐

close   enclose   enclosure ☐

Jane suffered from exposure when she was caught out in a blizzard. ☐

The disclosure of those secrets will cause a lot of trouble. ☐

My dog can get all of the sheep into the enclosure. ☐

sure   insure   insurance ☐

cure   secure   securely ☐

You should never drive a car without insurance. ☐

Please lock the door securely when you go to bed. ☐

> guess, guest, guitar, guard, guilty, guide, sign

My leg really hurts, but the nurse said there is no sign of a _____.

    feature   fraction   fracture

Have you measured the strings for your _____ ?

    guitar   station   vulture

You should always fasten your seat belt _____?

    securely   section   shortly

If you can't read that word, you should not try to _____.

    grief   piece   guess

The guards quickly recaptured the _____ people.

    guests   guilty   healthy

We ought to hire a _____ so we don't get lost on our adventure.

    great   goes   guide

All the married _____ hurried to attend the lecture.

    horses   ladies   goats

My father fought with the Welsh Guards in the _____.

    warning   warm   war

FLUENCY READING

☐ Pass: 10 sec.　☆ Bonus: 8 sec.　★ Double Bonus: 6 sec.

lawn	thud	pine	pause	☐ ☆ ★
bird	haunts	hay	reed	☐ ☆ ★
morse	bight	craw	because	☐ ☆ ★
coy	gale	crawl	flange	☐ ☆ ★
haunch	fort	stale	distance	☐ ☆ ★
saucer	cute	thick	vain	☐ ☆ ★
claw	lace	Gaul	catch	☐ ☆ ★
beer	daub	hinge	Eve	☐ ☆ ★
Maud	lark	burnt	gawk	☐ ☆ ★
trim	switches	foil	hair	☐ ☆ ★
faun	zone	gaunt	hurt	☐ ☆ ★
pert	prawn	smudge	sauce	☐ ☆ ★
fail	those	yawn	sir	☐ ☆ ★

> quiet, key

The Sign of the Vulture

With ten lighters in his pockets, Mark went off to find the door to the raw prawn hold. When he got below, he followed Sue's directions and found the right door. The pirates had put a huge padlock on the door, so there was nothing that Mark could do. He went back up on deck to the ventilation shaft, and gave Sue and Maud the bad news. "Don't let them capture you, my lad," Sue warned him. "They might decide to torture you. They are all thieves and cut-throats. You must go and hide before they all wake up, and Jolly Roger guesses you are missing."

Mark dropped nine of the lighters down the ventilation shaft and went to hide in the life-boat. The sun was rising in the east, and steam was rising from the smelly, drunken thieves who were passed out on the hard steel deck. Leif the chief thief was the smelliest of them all, for his head was still stuck in a pail of raw prawns.

Mark was very tired, and he slept until noon. When he woke up, the pirates were shouting and cursing. He heard Lief the chief thief say "But we must have more cider! My head hurts, and going without cider is pure torture!"

Jolly Roger shouted, "If you sail under the sign of the vulture, you must do as I say." Mark saw a flag flying from the highest mast, and it had a picture of a vulture on it. In story-books, pirates sailed under the skull-and-crossbones. He thought that times must have changed. Jolly Roger carried on with his lecture: "If I am the boss, we will find lots of treasure, and we will all be very wealthy. You are just drunken slobs who think only of pleasure. If we do not plan for the future, they will catch us and hang us from the yard-arm. Now get below and get some steam in the boilers, and then we will go off and search for treasure".

The pirates all grumbled, because they wanted to drink more cider. But they knew that Jolly Roger had a point. They did not want to be hung like dogs—even the dogs did not want that. But Leif the chief thief was standing next to the life-boat, and Mark heard him mutter to another pirate, "Who does he think he is? Yesterday, Jolly Roger was stuffing raw prawns in crates of ice, and now he believes he is some kind of god. We will see about that." With this, Leif the chief thief lit a cigar (for he still had forty lighters) and stomped away.

Do you think Sue and Maud are getting fed up with raw prawns?

Mastery Test

Any pupil who does not pass this test must go back to page 84. This is very important—a child who is struggling will not be learning. Contrary to what you would think, most children would rather go back than carry on getting things wrong. If the pupil needs to go back, use a different coloured pencil for ticking the boxes.

Use the cursor as you would on a Fluency Reading page.

Timed reading: 'Pass' mark is 15 seconds per line.

heaviest	reception	nature	preparing	☐
capture	relief	affectionate	married	☐
field	mixture	believe	stories	☐
chief	picture	ladies	adventure	☐

Reading accuracy: Pass mark is one mistake.

Do not prompt. You may allow the pupil to self correct, but you cannot say anything except "Try again".

Jane hurried home to see the new puppies. ☐

My niece was overcome with grief when a thief stole her television. ☐

Moving all that heavy furniture was pure torture. ☐

Our departure was delayed because a tyre was punctured.☐

Soft 'c':

If a pupil makes a mistake, back up the cursor and then sound out the word.

city	certain	circle	Cecil	cistern	☐
pencil	cycle	central	century	cedar	☐
council	fancy	fancied	special	cinnamon	☐

Please sign your name with the blue pencil. ☐

On warm days I like to cycle to school. ☐

Uncle Cecil fixed the leaking cistern in our bathroom. ☐

The English Civil War was fought in the seventeenth century. ☐

The council workers chopped down that nice cedar tree. ☐

Luke fancied some cinnamon buns as a special treat. ☐

centre	central	parcel	cinder	license	☐
cistern	acid	citizen	civic	centre	☐
spice	spicy	spiciest	social	cement	☐

The car Clive just bought has central locking. ☐

You can use this special cement for gluing rubber. ☐

Dawn boiled some acid in her kettle to remove the lime scale. ☐

You will need a passport if you are not a British citizen. ☐

Uncle Cecil makes the spiciest curries. ☐

They hold lots of social functions at the civic centre. ☐

DECODING POWER PAGE

Always use the cursor!

relaxation	television	sensation	injection	☐
adventure	exposure	insure	capture	☐
city	pencil	council	centre	☐
mummies	niece	relieve	thief	☐
circle	spice	certain	cycle	☐
caption	revision	restoration	pollution	☐
feature	disclosure	secure	enclosure	☐
fancy	central	acid	spicy	☐
placing	ripen	dozy	hoping	☐
yield	scarier	ladies	achieve	☐
civil	parcel	citizen	Cecil	☐
measure	recapture	fracture	vulture	☐
rifle	cradle	tumble	pickle	☐
spiciest	fancied	cinder	cement	☐
reception	ventilation	permission	information	☐
license	cistern	special	cinnamon	☐
lecture	treasure	closure	culture	☐
cedar	social	century	civic	☐

Wordbuilder

Do not award ticks for a 'good try'—your pupil will pay for it later!

cern	concern	concerning		☐
cel	excel	excellent	excellently	☐
vent	advent	adventure	adventurous	☐
cide	decide	decided	undecided	☐
place	replace	replacing		☐

Bruce just got a letter concerning his driving license. ☐

I thought Peter's picture of a vulture was excellent. ☐

Charles is still excited about his great adventure. ☐

Jean is quite undecided about replacing her furniture. ☐

cent	recent	recently		☐
cess	success	successful	unsuccessful	☐
lay	layer	bricklayer		☐
cise	precise	precisely		☐
ceive	receive	received		☐

The search for the guilty thieves was unsuccessful. ☐

Bricklayers mix sand and cement to make mortar. ☐

The train's departure will be at six o'clock precisely. ☐

Dawn recently received a large parcel in the post. ☐

| young, country, couple, touch, laugh, build, built |

Spain and France are the only _____ I have visited.

    countries   couples   curries

The smooth texture of silk is a pleasure to _____.

    teach   torch   touch

My Uncle Cecil used to _____ as a builder.

    guard   worry   work

Steve only _____ at the funniest jokes.

    looks   laughs   signs

These puppies are too _____ to leave their mother.

    young   great   healthy

The young _____ had to get a special license to get married.

    country   collie   couple

In this country, most houses are _____ from bricks and cement.

    bought   built   believed

Luke is too _____ to draw social security payments.

    dead   young   poor

FLUENCY READING

☐ Pass: 10 sec. ☆ Bonus: 8 sec. ☆ Double Bonus: 6 sec.

taught	sore	cord	drove	☐ ☆ ☆
burning	brawn	launch	soap	☐ ☆ ☆
nude	Bruce	shape	Dutch	☐ ☆ ☆
more	flit	boarder	midge	☐ ☆ ☆
jade	jeep	goal	bright	☐ ☆ ☆
stab	hawk	reserve	wore	☐ ☆ ☆
Crete	fawn	stem	surf	☐ ☆ ☆
mock	crime	trudge	crude	☐ ☆ ☆
tuneful	coach	pair	blight	☐ ☆ ☆
ripe	hutch	dime	beech	☐ ☆ ☆
daub	patches	shade	spawn	☐ ☆ ☆
coin	stole	merge	rope	☐ ☆ ☆
slight	fair	harsh	gripe	☐ ☆ ☆

Cecil the Special Civet

Mark thought that he ought to do something about Leif the chief thief. He was worried because Leif might try to capture Jolly Roger and throw him in the raw prawn hold with Sue the gruesome stoker. Sailing under the sign of the vulture was no laughing matter, but it would certainly be far worse if Leif the chief thief took over. The pirates would drink cider all day, and drunken pirates are not very nice.

Mark was lying in the bottom of the life-boat trying to find a comfortable position when a small creature caught his attention. "Shhh! Be quiet", it said. "I am Cecil, the special civet. I am hiding from the pirates, too." Mark said, "I hate to be rude, but I am not sure that I have ever met a special civet before. What do special civets do?"

Cecil stroked his silky whiskers. "Well," he said, "civets are cat-like creatures that live in cedar trees and eat cinnamon toast." Cecil had a quick glance around to be sure that there were no pirates about. "But I'll tell you what special civets are really for. When a writer isn't sure what to do with his story, he throws in a special civet. All good writers have lots of special civets."

"Well," Mark said, "I hope you know what to do with these pirates. You can get a bad reputation if you sail under the sign of the vulture. And I really am worried about Sue, the gruesome stoker. She is locked in the raw prawn hold with Maudlin Maud and Nate the first mate. Neal the real seal is there too, except I don't think he will mind being locked up in the raw prawn hold, because he is a seal."

Cecil smoothed his whiskers (for special civets are rather vain) and thought for a while. Then he said, "I think I have the solution. We will wait until it is dark, and then we will sneak up to Maud's cabin. We ought to find Jolly Roger there, because he is in charge of this trawler. You can make a distraction, while I sneak in his cabin and find the keys to the raw prawn hold. Then I will unlock the raw prawn hold, and Sue the gruesome stoker will feed Jolly Roger to the sharks."

Mark said, "That is a good plan, but if I make a distraction, the pirates are bound to catch me. Are you sure that you can find the keys? Unless we can get Sue out of the raw prawn hold, the pirates will certainly capture me. And I do not want to be tortured."

Do you think Cecil has eaten all of his cinnamon toast?

'y' to 'i':

If a pupil makes a mistake, back up the cursor and then sound out the word.

try	tries	tried	dry	drier	driest	☐
cry	cries	cried	fly	flies	flier	☐
fry	fries	fried	spy	spies	spied	☐

No matter how hard we tried, we could not score a goal. ☐

Do you like your eggs boiled or fried? ☐

If your shirt is still wet, just put it in the tumble drier. ☐

Jess cries a lot when she watches sad films. ☐

pry	pries	pried	ply	plies	plied	☐
ply	apply	applied	ply	imply	implied	☐
ply	reply	replies	ply	supply	supplies	☐
try	retry	retried	deny	denied		☐

Steve thought that Spike stole his bike but Spike denied it. ☐

Drew applied for a job working for a builder. ☐

Roy always tries his best to avoid any trouble at school. ☐

You should never eat anything that is covered with flies. ☐

Uncle Cecil wrote me a letter last week, but I still haven't replied. ☐

In the States, chips are called French fries. ☐

We bought our supplies before we went camping. ☐

DECODING POWER PAGE

Always use the cursor!

studies	field	curries	thieves	☐
civic	acid	cement	cedar	☐
tries	cried	replies	driest	☐
creature	mixture	treasure	puncture	☐
flier	spied	pries	fried	☐
scariest	carried	grief	siege	☐
cycle	pencil	Nancy	race	☐
drier	tried	replied	plies	☐
affection	nation	civilisation	fashion	☐
departure	exposure	secure	texture	☐
denied	pliable	fries	plied	☐
license	citizen	century	precise	☐
tidal	baby	final	tubing	☐
implies	flies	pried	supplies	☐
jungle	rustle	ladle	wrinkle	☐
cries	applied	spies	implied	☐
decide	concern	success	parcel	☐
retried	driest	supplied	denies	☐

Wordbuilder

Do not award ticks for a 'good try'—your pupil will pay for it later!

note	notify	notified		☐
sate	satisfy	satisfied	unsatisfied	☐
drive	driver	screwdriver		☐
build	building	rebuilding		☐
ceed	succeed	succeeding		☐

When were you notified of the change of dates? ☐

Some people are never satisfied. ☐

Luke pried the lid off the tin of paint with a screwdriver. ☐

They are rebuilding the old church because it was falling to pieces. ☐

You must try harder if you do not succeed at first. ☐

cent	recent	recently		☐
civil	civilise	civilisation		☐
sign	assign	assignment		☐
plore	explore	explorer	explorers	☐
cover	discover	discovery	discoveries	☐
cite	excite	exciting		☐

We learned about Greek civilisation from this assignment. ☐

Explorers have made many exciting discoveries recently. ☐

111

> rough, tough, enough, busy, eight, police

We will take a _____ at eight o'clock.

    sign   break   guess

When you play with a young kitten, you should not be too _____.

    round   rough   laugh

During the Great War, the ____ were busy looking for spies.

    police   builders   couples

They have not supplied _____ bricks to build our house.

    tough   eight   enough

Jake thinks he is _____, but he is really a wimp.

    guilty   tough   busy

I am not satisfied that you have _____ hard enough.

    tried   fried   implied

Spike applied to join the police, but he wasn't _____.

    accepted   expected   excited

If you put bricks in your tumble drier, it might _____.

    build   break   bought

FLUENCY READING

☐ Pass: 10 sec. ☆ Bonus: 8 sec. ★ Double Bonus: 6 sec.

aired	switch	shed	may	☐ ☆ ★
wedge	mine	paw	witch	☐ ☆ ★
cheer	mime	yaw	dive	☐ ☆ ★
squirt	terse	pay	shun	☐ ☆ ★
botch	shame	charm	jeer	☐ ☆ ★
budge	game	ketch	cone	☐ ☆ ★
quack	yawn	flirting	slope	☐ ☆ ★
pope	bay	roar	blue	☐ ☆ ★
burn	Kew	page	shut	☐ ☆ ★
Roy	drew	grip	kitchen	☐ ☆ ★
mew	board	chock	launder	☐ ☆ ★
fuel	plate	unload	toil	☐ ☆ ★
due	trade	few	awful	☐ ☆ ★

> moustache

The Secret Policeman

When it got dark, Cecil the special civet prepared to go to the rescue of Sue the gruesome stoker. Mark saw him stick a false moustache over his whiskers, and asked "Why are you doing that?" Cecil replied, "Special civets are really secret policemen. We have to go out in disguise so people won't know that we are cops." With this, Cecil applied some bright red lipstick. "Now you would never guess that I am a special civet, let alone a policeman." he said.

"Now we must think of a disguise for you," Cecil said. "We ought to disguise you as a little boy—you almost look tough enough to be a boy. Let's get busy and find a disguise for you." Cecil started digging into the containers that were stored in the lifeboat. "Great!" he cried, "Here is a guitar. Now you can pretend you are a rock star. And here is a chain! Rock stars must have chains in their noses. There—you look just fine."

Mark did not like to have a heavy chain hanging from his nose, and the guitar was almost big enough to sleep in. But as soon as it was dark enough, they crawled out of the life-boat. A guitar string got caught, and it made a horrible "PLONNNK". "Shhh!" Cecil whispered, "You must be quiet, or the pirates will find us. How do we get to Maud's cabin?" Mark knew that Maud's cabin was just behind the bridge, so he led Cecil up the ladder to the bridge. They crept across the bridge, being careful not to wake up Amanda the giant panda. She was asleep at the wheel, and the trawler was sailing around in circles.

Cecil and Mark crept up to Maud's cabin. The door was closed, but they could hear Scary Mary shouting, "What kind of pirate do you call yourself, Jolly Roger? You have been in charge of this tub for a full day now, and you have not made one single person walk the plank. You have not fed anyone to the sharks, and you have not captured any treasure ships. All your men are muttering and cursing because they want the cider. If you don't watch yourself, Lief the chief thief will take over. And I have half a mind to help him, you spineless worm!"

Outside the door, Cecil nudged Mark. "It sounds like all is not well under the sign of the vulture." Cecil whispered. "Now is the time to make a commotion. Rock stars are good at that."

Do you think that Scary Mary is very good natured?

Mastery Test

Any pupil who does not pass this test must go back to page 101. This is very important—a child who is struggling will not be learning. Contrary to what you would think, most children would rather go back than carry on getting things wrong. If the pupil needs to go back, use a different coloured pencil for ticking the boxes.

Use the cursor as you would on a Fluency Reading page.

Timed reading: 'Pass' mark is 15 seconds per line.

central	excellent	supplies	special	☐
screwdriver	fries	century	distraction	☐
precisely	succeeding	cried	social	☐
license	replied	parcel	cement	☐

Reading accuracy: Pass mark is one mistake.
Do not prompt. You may allow the pupil to self correct, but you cannot say anything except "Try again".

Clive fancied cinnamon buns washed down with cider. ☐

Explorers have made some exciting discoveries recently. ☐

We are not satisfied with our new tumble drier. ☐

Cecil has applied to become a British citizen. ☐

Dancing Bears

Well done!

You have completed
Level 9

You are now working on Level 10

-age

If a pupil makes a mistake, back up the cursor and then sound out the word.

postage   package   cottage   village   marriage   ☐

luggage   voyage   coverage   breakage   baggage   ☐

How much postage do you need for that package?   ☐

There are five thatched cottages in our village.   ☐

My mother and father have a very happy marriage.   ☐

How much luggage can I take on this voyage?   ☐

bandage   garbage   shortage   cabbage   drainage   ☐

manage   sausage   wreckage   blockage   passage   ☐

Put all the used bandages in with the garbage.   ☐

There was a shortage of cabbages last winter.   ☐

Our yard is muddy because the drainage is bad.   ☐

Do you think you could manage another sausage?   ☐

salvage   damage   vintage   voltage   message   ☐

language   sewage   silage   savage   rampage   ☐

We can salvage your car if the damage is not too bad.   ☐

The headlights on vintage cars have low voltage.   ☐

He left a message in some strange language.   ☐

Sewage smells even worse than silage.   ☐

DECODING ~ POWER ~ PAGE

Do not award ticks for a 'good try'—your pupil will pay for it later!

pasture	future	nature	feature	☐
tried	pries	applies	supplier	☐
village	garbage	message	postage	☐
special	central	social	cistern	☐
package	voyage	blockage	vintage	☐
posture	cure	pleasure	torture	☐
retries	flier	plied	driest	☐
savage	passage	cottage	luggage	☐
diversion	intention	sensation	pension	☐
cinnamon	cinder	success	recent	☐
drainage	shortage	manage	salvage	☐
relies	fried	retried	pliable	☐
securing	usable	fury	latest	☐
damage	cabbage	breakage	baggage	☐
pure	picture	insure	creature	☐
marriage	sausage	bandage	voltage	☐
denial	applies	drier	spied	☐
wreckage	rampage	coverage	sewage	☐

Wordbuilder

Always use the cursor!

close   enclose   enclosure ☐

broke   broken   unbroken ☐

cide   *accide*   accident   accidental   accidentally ☐

cover   recover   recovering ☐

ease   disease   diseased ☐

All those glasses were broken accidentally. ☐

My uncle is still recovering from a nasty disease. ☐

When we have finished riding, we put our horses back
in the enclosure. ☐

cess   necessary   unnecessary   unnecessarily ☐

mit   commit   committee ☐

miss   mission   permission ☐

fine   final   finally ☐

count   counter   encounter   encountered ☐

vent   event   eventful   eventfully   uneventfully ☐

I hate all this unnecessary homework. ☐

The day passed uneventfully and we were all bored. ☐

The planning committee finally gave us permission to put
up a fence. ☐

Yesterday we encountered some friends on our walk
in the park. ☐

| bear, wear, tear, swear, lie, tie, pie |

Did you get enough _____ pie?

    cabbage   cottage   sewage

Do you have to wear a ___ to school?

    sausage   sign   tie

Have you seen any bears _____?

    dancing   flying   laughing

Our cabbages all ____ of some strange blight.

    died   fried   spied

Bart was expelled from school for _____ at a teacher.

    swearing   tearing   wearing

If you are tired, you _____ to go and lie down.

    thought   should   ought

James could hardly wait to ____ open the package.

    tough   touch   tear

Uncle Cecil bought some vintage wines at an _____.

    action   auction   adventure

FLUENCY READING

☐ Pass: 10 sec.   ☆ Bonus: 8 sec.   ★ Double Bonus: 6 sec.

roar	clue	skirmish	flew	☐ ☆ ★
slime	march	yore	lodge	☐ ☆ ★
true	tawny	skew	coal	☐ ☆ ★
flit	explode	chew	five	☐ ☆ ★
harp	yew	new	lice	☐ ☆ ★
fair	coil	brew	Luke	☐ ☆ ★
fright	newt	herb	applaud	☐ ☆ ★
hue	wife	disgrace	boar	☐ ☆ ★
pew	came	stew	shawl	☐ ☆ ★
oil	shorn	Sue	turf	☐ ☆ ★
rue	ode	queer	scotch	☐ ☆ ★
glue	drawn	grew	lay	☐ ☆ ★
rule	predate	flue	hew	☐ ☆ ★

Mark's rock concert

Amanda the giant panda snored loudly as she slumped over the wheel, and the trawler carried on sailing around in tight little circles. Cecil the special civet told Mark, "I will go and hide behind the door, and then you must start playing your guitar. As soon as Jolly Roger and Scary Mary come out to see who is making all the noise, I will slip into their cabin and steal the keys to the raw prawn hold."

Mark could barely manage to lift the guitar, let alone play it. But he thought that if Froid the pet snail could play a guitar, then so could he. He put his fingers on the strings and started strumming. Amanda woke up, but she fell to the deck with an almighty crash and knocked herself out. The cabin door swung open, and Jolly Roger and Scary Mary came out.

"What on earth is all this commotion?" shouted Scary Mary. "I am a rock star," Mark mumbled, "and I came here to entertain you. Life on a rusty old trawler can be awfully boring." Jolly Roger said, "Well, I don't care much for rock. I prefer garage myself."

Scary Mary heard a noise, and she turned her head a bit. "Jolly Roger, can't you do anything right? The cat has just got out!" Jolly Roger replied, "But we haven't got a cat. I swear we haven't." Scary Mary said, "Don't lie to me, Jolly Roger, or you will die. I just saw a cat running out of the cabin. He was wearing a moustache and bright red lipstick. I don't know what you do to your pets. Dressing them up is cruel."

While they were arguing, Mark slipped out from behind the guitar and started to sneak away. He had to crawl over Amanda's huge body, but she was snoring so loudly that Scary Mary and Jolly Roger did not hear him escape. He went down the ladder to the main deck, and then down the hatch to the raw prawn hold. Cecil the special civet was there, trying to open the lock. His moustache had slipped, so that now he was wearing a false beard. "Dear me," he said, "none of these keys work."

Do you think cats should wear red lipstick?

Soft 'g'

If a pupil makes a mistake, back up the cursor and then sound out the word.

strange   stranger   danger   change   changed   ☐

changing   gentle   gerbil   magic   gypsy   ☐

The stranger changed our tyre very quickly.   ☐

In time of war, a spy lives a life of great danger.   ☐

Please be gentle with my gerbil.   ☐

I like to watch the gypsy perform her magic show.   ☐

gesture   giant   George   German   general   ☐

You should never make rude gestures at a giant.   ☐

King George was our first German king.   ☐

Some people think that General Studies are a waste of time.   ☐

midge   genius   geniuses   gently   gadget   ☐

ginger   gin   register   college   algebra   ☐

Our kitchen is full of useless gadgets.   ☐

A midge is a very small insect.   ☐

You must play very gently with a young kitten.   ☐

Uncle Cecil likes to relax with a glass of gin and ginger ale.   ☐

In the Great War, many German generals were geniuses.   ☐

Our teacher has already taken the register.   ☐

DECODING ~ POWER ~ PAGE

Do not award ticks for a 'good try'—your pupil will pay for it later!

excel	decide	civil	cycle	☐
cottage	blockage	silage	language	☐
strange	changing	gesture	midget	☐
fries	cried	denies	replied	☐
ginger	danger	magic	gypsy	☐
succeed	civic	accident	special	☐
postage	luggage	bandage	manage	☐
change	gerbil	George	gin	☐
insurance	departure	exposure	capture	☐
relied	implies	spied	pliers	☐
gentle	stranger	giant	gadget	☐
package	voyage	garbage	sausage	☐
babies	noisiest	priest	thieves	☐
changed	German	genius	college	☐
Cecil	centre	necessary	century	☐
general	register	algebra	fidget	☐
coverage	shortage	wreckage	vintage	☐
gently	lodger	image	geniuses	☐

Wordbuilder

Always use the cursor!

gent	gentle	gentlemen		☐
urge	urgent	urgently		☐
quest	request	requested		☐
gest	suggest	suggestion		☐

All gentlemen are urgently requested to make some suggestions. ☐

image	imagine	imaginary		☐
gest	digest	digestion	indigestion	☐
gine	engine	engineer	engineering	☐
logic	logical	logically	illogically	☐

Many young children have imaginary friends. ☐

If you eat too fast, you are sure to get indigestion. ☐

My uncle George studied engineering in college. ☐

Studying algebra teaches you to think logically. ☐

cide	decide	decided	undecided	☐
cept	accept	acceptable	unacceptable	☐
gin	origin	original	originally	☐
gest	suggest	suggestion		☐

We have decided to accept your original suggestion. ☐

> young, country, couple, touch, laugh, build, built

Our Uncle George built a house in the _____ .

    couple   caution   country

Please don't touch my guitar—you might _____ it.

    manage   damage   salvage

Maud studied algebra in _____ .

    cottage   college   cabbage

The builders have just laid the _____ for our new cottage.

    foundations   suggestions   digestion

No matter how hard I tried, I never managed to speak _____ .

    gerbil   general   German

The young genius had many original _____.

    laughs   ideas   lies

You ought to pay more attention to your mother's _____.

    imagination   gadgets   suggestions

Is Spike tough enough to _____ down the door?

    break   busy   bear

FLUENCY READING

☐ Pass: 10 sec.   ☆ Bonus: 8 sec.   ★ Double Bonus: 6 sec.

dosh	gore	street	scrape	☐ ☆ ★
split	scrawl	oak	stretch	☐ ☆ ★
gruel	churn	thrash	serve	☐ ☆ ★
sprite	squint	skewer	ketch	☐ ☆ ★
deer	poach	shrimp	argue	☐ ☆ ★
throne	grill	Norse	screed	☐ ☆ ★
straw	scram	Jew	hoard	☐ ☆ ★
stage	squeeze	throve	three	☐ ☆ ★
nail	seep	spew	splodge	☐ ☆ ★
spring	cue	leer	shrub	☐ ☆ ★
strive	strip	paunch	Tay	☐ ☆ ★
throb	trews	squirt	strut	☐ ☆ ★
lock	shrine	lore	shred	☐ ☆ ★

George the German Gerbil

Cecil the special civet had taken the wrong keys, so he could not open the door to the raw prawn hold. Mark went to the ventilation shaft so he could give the bad news to Sue the gruesome stoker. Sue was disappointed, and she said, "You must go down to the boiler room and look under the pile of oily rags. That is where George the German gerbil lives. He is very shy, but he is a genius. Tell him you have a message from Sue. If you give him a spicy sausage, he will trust you."

Mark turned away from the ventilation shaft and saw Scary Mary chasing Cecil the special civet with a broom. "You horrible cat!" she shouted, "You stole my cinnamon toast. If I ever manage to catch you, I will make you into cat stew!" But Cecil was too quick for Scary Mary, and he ran up the mast. Mark took advantage of this distraction to slip off to the boiler room.

Leif the chief thief was supposed to be stoking the boilers, but he had fallen asleep. The fire in the boiler was almost out, and the trawler was dead in the water again. Mark took a few lighters from Leif's pockets, and he didn't twitch. So Mark guessed it was safe to talk to George the German gerbil. He went to the pile of oily rags and whispered, "I have a message from Sue. She said you would like a spicy sausage, but even if I could find one I would have eaten it myself, for I am a very, very hungry boy. But Sue said you were a genius, and you would know what to do."

A little furry nose poked out from under the oily rags. A tiny pair of glasses was perched on that nose, for gerbils are very short-sighted. "Yes, I am a genius," said George, "but I am very shy. I will have to hide in your dress or I will not leave the boiler room."

So Mark took George the German gerbil and tucked him under his dress. George was covered in shredded newspaper, for he was a gerbil. Mark told him everything that had happened, and then George replied, "Why it is all very simple. I have a plan that will save us all. First, we must go and get your friend Cecil down from the mast. Secret policemen are good at climbing up things, but they are not so good at getting down. Once we get him down, I will tell you what we can do."

Do you think that gerbils speak with a German accent?

Mastery Test

Any pupil who does not pass this test must go back to page 119. This is very important—a child who is struggling will not be learning. Contrary to what you would think, most children would rather go back than carry on getting things wrong. If the pupil needs to go back, use a different coloured pencil for ticking the boxes.

Use the cursor as you would on a Fluency Reading page.

Timed reading: 'Pass' mark is 15 seconds per line.

gentleman	magic	accident	cottage	☐
shortage	suggestion	gerbil	committee	☐
package	voyage	logical	gadget	☐
register	garbage	bandage	original	☐

Reading accuracy: Pass mark is one mistake.

Do not prompt. You may allow the pupil to self correct, but you cannot say anything except "Try again".

You should never make rude gestures at a German giant. ☐

Could you manage some more sausages and cabbage? ☐

Do geniuses generally drink gin and ginger beer? ☐

The caller left a message in some strange language. ☐

Hard 'ch', ph

Do not award ticks for a 'good try'—your pupil will pay for it later!

phone   telephone   photo   photograph   ☐

physical   physics   dolphin   alphabet   ☐

pheasant   orphan   nephew   elephant   ☐

Sue fancies taking some photos of the elephant. ☐

I tried to reach you on your cell phone, but it was busy. ☐

You can't learn to read if you don't learn the alphabet. ☐

In the country, many gentlemen shoot pheasants. ☐

Peter tries to get some physical exercise every day. ☐

school   Christmas   stomach   ache   ☐

chemist   chemistry   mechanic   technical   ☐

schooner   scheme   character   anchor   ☐

Steve came home from school with a stomach ache. ☐

Marge always gets enough presents for Christmas. ☐

The chemist can give you some pills to relieve your indigestion. ☐

I believe that Arthur studied chemistry in school. ☐

Maud sailed on a schooner to see the dolphins. ☐

Martin learned how to be a mechanic at technical college. ☐

The ship rode out the storm at anchor. ☐

DECODING POWER PAGE

Always use the cursor!

tried	reliable	denial	supplies	☐
urgent	suggest	imagine	digest	☐
phone	chemist	pheasant	school	☐
salvage	village	voltage	language	☐
schedule	physical	Christmas	orphan	☐
retries	pries	undeniable	driest	☐
engine	logic	origin	gadget	☐
chemistry	photo	scheme	dolphin	☐
necessary	access	cycle	cinnamon	☐
damage	sewage	breakage	cabbage	☐
nephew	stomach	physics	mechanic	☐
changes	German	college	gently	☐
rapture	feature	rupture	nature	☐
character	physics	ache	alphabet	☐
permission	auction	commotion	digestion	☐
elephant	technical	photograph	anchor	☐
register	ginger	gerbil	magic	☐
chemical	dolphin	orphan	Chris	☐

137

Wordbuilder

If your pupil makes a mistake, back up the cursor and sound out the word.

cern   concern   concerning   □

photo   photograph   photographic   □

quip   equip   equipment   □

pense   expense   expensive   inexpensive   □

vent   venture   adventure   adventurous   □

dure   endure   endurance   □

Photographic equipment can be very expensive.   □

This adventure holiday will be a real test of endurance.   □

lieve   believe   believable   unbelievable   unbelievably   □

gust   disgust   disgusting   disgustingly   □

muse   amuse   amusing   amusingly   □

verse   converse   conversation   □

Their curries are unbelievably disgusting.   □

Mother had an amusing conversation with her nephew.   □

rupt   disrupt   disruption   disruptions   □

cess   necessary   unnecessary   □

A naughty child can cause a lot of disruption at school.   □

I hate all this unnecessary homework.   □

> fruit, juice, suit, cruise, bruise, island

Uncle George went on a ____ to Christmas Island.

    cruise   choose   shoot

Did you get enough fruit ____ to drink?

    junk   Joyce   juice

My Uncle Cecil has to wear a ____ and tie to work.

    search   sign   suit

If you play ____ games, you might get a bruise.

    bear   rough   break

Our ____ only works on German cars.

    mechanic   chemist   character

The police caught the thieves ____ into our garage.

    breaking   building   swearing

You ought to pick some ____ so we can bake a pie.

    juice   fruit   idea

Which suit did Carl wear when he got ____?

    worried   hurried   married

FLUENCY READING

☐ Pass: 10 sec.   ☆ Bonus: 8 sec.   ★ Double Bonus: 6 sec.

duel	tight	splat	soy	☐ ☆ ★
slew	thrill	grate	scrimp	☐ ☆ ★
cheek	August	spruce	value	☐ ☆ ★
quince	lair	splint	flute	☐ ☆ ★
thrip	blue	quoin	scratch	☐ ☆ ★
scruffy	thwack	male	par	☐ ☆ ★
dewy	Jude	awe	expose	☐ ☆ ★
oar	waif	stripe	awning	☐ ☆ ★
pride	Tuesday	wick	Jane	☐ ☆ ★
waiter	bulge	fail	bairn	☐ ☆ ★
scrumpy	muse	cruel	dislike	☐ ☆ ★
lain	quid	staunch	became	☐ ☆ ★
shrank	maudlin	chore	unsafe	☐ ☆ ★

Liberation At Last

Mark tucked George the German gerbil firmly inside his dress and went back up on deck. Scary Mary had got tired of chasing Cecil the special civet and was nowhere to be seen. Cecil was still perched on top of the mast. German George the gerbil said to Mark, "Well, we can't very well call out the fire brigade. You must ask Cecil to drop his keys down to us."

After Mark did this, Cecil said, "Why certainly you can have the keys, but please do not forget and leave me up here. Secret policemen simply cannot climb down backwards, our tails get in the way."

George said to Mark, "Now we will set my scheme into action. Let us go and unlock the cider store, and the rum store too. After that, we will go down to the boiler room and tell Leif the chief thief. He will be delighted with the news."

Very soon, all the pirates were roaring drunk again. Jolly Roger and Scary Mary came down from the bridge and shouted, but none of the pirates paid any attention to them. Mark and George were hiding in the anchor locker, and George said, "Now is our chance. We must hurry up to their cabin and get the keys to the raw prawn hold. Jolly Roger has hidden them in the toilet cistern." Mark was amazed. "How do you know that?" he asked. George tapped his furry little nose and said, "I am a genius. That is how I know."

Mark raced up to the cabin and lifted the lid on the toilet cistern. Sure enough, there was a key wired to the ballcock.

He hurried down to the raw prawn hold, and much to his surprise, the key opened the lock. Sue the gruesome stoker rushed out and hugged Mark in her big beefy arms. "Mark my lad, you have saved the day again. I certainly hope you have had some lunch." Poor George (the German gerbil) was still tucked in Mark's dress, and they could hear him squeak, "Help! you should never crush a genius!"

Sue stormed up to the main deck, followed by Maud, Nate, Neal and the loyal crew. Sue bellowed out, "You have a choice. You can take your rum and cider down to the raw prawn hold, or I will throw you to the sharks." The pirates were frozen with fear. Sue stared Leif the chief thief right in the eye and started towards him. Suddenly all the pirates started grabbing kegs of cider and rum and running down to the raw prawn hold.

Do you think everyone has forgotten Cecil?

> **-ion:**

Always use the cursor!

motion   promotion   emotion   reflection   section   ☐

You must hold on tightly while the train is in motion. ☐

Bruce works very hard and he deserves a promotion. ☐

You should never get carried away by your emotions. ☐

I can see your reflection in the mirror. ☐

Have you read the sports section of the newspaper yet? ☐

admission   explosion   collision   election   mansion   ☐

The police might take your words as an admission of guilt. ☐

The gas explosion woke us up at eight o'clock. ☐

Clive didn't have a chance of avoiding that collision. ☐

My Uncle Cecil votes in every election. ☐

Do all pop stars live in huge mansions? ☐

partition   division   population suspicion   aviation   ☐

My father built a partition across our bedroom to stop us fighting. ☐

A good maths teacher can explain how to do long division. ☐

France and Britain have roughly the same population. ☐

I have a suspicion that our cat is the thief. ☐

Tim studies aviation because he wants to join the Royal Air Force. ☐

DECODING ⚡ POWER ⚡ PAGE

If a pupil makes a mistake, back up the cursor and then sound out the word.

silage	marriage	baggage	drainage	☐
alphabet	anchor	telephone	scheme	☐
elephant	ache	nephew	character	☐
motion	section	admission	partition	☐
original	suggestion	engineer	midget	☐
reflection	explosion	division	emotion	☐
passage	savage	message	rampage	☐
photograph	technical	school	physics	☐
collision	population	promotion	election	☐
spies	flier	pliable	supplier	☐
giant	magical	genius	algebra	☐
mansion	division	suspicion	aviation	☐
chemistry	physical	Chris	pheasant	☐
exciting	civilise	access	decide	☐
conclusion	liberation	disruption	conversation	☐
postage	voyage	wreckage	carriage	☐
distraction	caution	foundation	digestion	☐
photo	schedule	dolphin	stomach	☐

Wordbuilder

Do not award ticks for a 'good try'—your pupil will pay for it later!

form   inform   information ☐

stand   understand   understanding ☐

dict   dictate   dictation ☐

What is the use of all this information if you don't understand it? ☐

We had to write ten lines from dictation. ☐

fect   perfect   perfection   perfectionist ☐

exam   examine   examination ☐

cess   success   successful   successfully ☐

Steve takes forever because he is such a perfectionist. ☐

Jess sat her examinations successfully. ☐

ploy   employ   employed   unemployed ☐

port   transport   transportation ☐

mend   commend   recommend   recommendation ☐

Jake is still unemployed because he has no transportation. ☐

I can you give your friend a recommendation. ☐

rect   direct   direction   directions ☐

lead   leading   misleading ☐

We got lost because our directions were misleading. ☐

> bear, wear, tear, swear, lie, tie, pie

The flowers all died after the heavy _____ .

    fought   trouble   frost

I could swear that the thief was _____ a blue suit.

    warning   wearing   warming

The pirates hid their _____ on a lonely island.

    treasure   trouble   smarties

That photograph of me was so bad that I decided to ___ it up.

    tie   tear   sign

Does he always get caught out telling ___?

    flies   lies   tries

The bridge was built to ____ a heavy load.

    bear   bought   break

This woollen cloth feels rough to the ____ .

    tough   torch   touch

It only hurts when I _____.

    lunch   laugh   lurk

FLUENCY READING

☐ Pass: 10 sec.   ☆ Bonus: 8 sec.   ★ Double Bonus: 6 sec.

strew	wifely	sprayed	quern	☐ ☆ ★
brace	smartly	splutter	skate	☐ ☆ ★
bait	exclude	fewer	shrunken	☐ ☆ ★
redrawn	wisely	morn	thrip	☐ ☆ ★
defraud	shameless	hewn	reel	☐ ☆ ★
beginning	thrush	quid	prepay	☐ ☆ ★
pore	check	strapless	spiteful	☐ ☆ ★
strew	scrunch	tail	gaunt	☐ ☆ ★
useful	splitting	dawned	cork	☐ ☆ ★
unmade	clue	foam	sprightly	☐ ☆ ★
seer	thick	grunge	throaty	☐ ☆ ★
screw	shrill	queen	unwise	☐ ☆ ★
thaw	strewing	ensue	screed	☐ ☆ ★

Conclusion: Lunch!

All of the pirates were safely locked in the raw prawn hold when Mark said, "Has anyone seen Scary Mary? She must be hiding somewhere." Then Scary Mary crawled out of the lifeboat. She was holding the gun that Mark had hidden. "Now you will pay, Gruesome Sue," she sneered. "Now I will feed you and that horrible little girl to the sharks. If you do not jump over the side, I will shoot you both. Get moving!" she screamed. Mark laughed. "Go ahead and shoot," he said. "I am not afraid of you."

Mark walked slowly towards Scary Mary. She started shaking. "I'll shoot! I really will!" she screamed. She could not believe that this little child was walking towards her. She edged back, and then she tripped on an empty cider keg. Gruesome Sue rushed in and grabbed the gun and threw it over the side. She picked up Scary Mary by the scruff of the neck and carried her down to the raw prawn hold, and locked her up with the rest of the pirates. Nate the first mate hauled down the sign of the vulture, and gave it to Mark. "After all you have done, you certainly deserve to keep this." Cecil the special civet was still at the top of the mast, crying out, "You can't leave a secret policeman up here!"

Soon the trawler was back to normal. Maudlin Maud was on the bridge, crying for joy now that she had her trawler back. Nate the first mate was barking orders, and Neal the real seal was getting ready to trawl for more prawns. Gruesome Sue was down in the boiler room with Mark, and after they got the fires going again they sat down for a mug of sweet tea. George the German gerbil was back in his pile of oily rags, happily shredding up newspaper. "You are a very brave lad, Mark. How could you be sure she wouldn't pull the trigger?"

Mark said, "I couldn't be sure. But I knew the gun was empty, because I checked it after I took it from Jolly Roger." Sue laughed. "Well, you are still a brave boy. Now we have the boilers going, you must go and get some lunch. You must be very hungry by now."

So Mark went up to the bridge to see if he could get some lunch. The mess decks were empty, because Amanda the giant panda and Scary Mary were both locked up in the raw prawn hold. Just as he came up on the bridge, the lookout shouted, "Ahoy! There is a boat just ahead. It looks like a hunch-backed horse is rowing it!" Mark rushed to the rail, and sure enough, there was Hank. He was still in the boat that belonged to Smudge, the batty cat in the flat cap. Mark said, "That is Hank the hunch-backed horse, and he is an old mate of mine. I'll bet he is lost". Maud stopped the trawler and Hank came alongside.

Mark was really glad to see Hank again. Hank said, "Floyd the faultless fish is always getting lost. I have been rowing for days, and I am rather thirsty. Do you have any fruit juice?"

After he had a drink, Hank told them about an island he had found. Maud said, "I think we will go to that island and leave the pirates there. Then they can dig for treasure until the coast guard or the police pick them up!" Maud laughed for the first time on this cruise.

Mark asked if he could have some lunch. Maud said, "Why you can have anything you like. I think the fridge is still full of food." Mark said, "I have been in the fridge, and all the food is a year or two past its use-by date. Is there nothing else to eat?" Nate the first mate said, "I will share my last tin of dog food with you. I think it is rabbit and turkey." At last, Hank said, "Why don't you just turn back your watch? Sooner or later, you will get back to some place where there is some good food." Mark replied, "What a good idea. But I must say goodbye to Sue the gruesome stoker first."

Soon Mark was back at the pub, but Dawn had nothing but hedgehog crisps for him to eat. He turned his watch back again, and next they were at the church by the strange bridge. Smudge, the batty cat with the flat cap, had nothing but freshly-caught mice to feed him. Next, they got on the train set that belonged to Mike the loan shark. The first-class carriage was very comfortable, but the large man with a badge was out of cakes.

Mark turned back the hands again, and they were in the junk cars by the creepy marsh, but Jake the fake snake had run away with Groan, the croaking toad. Then at last he got back to Bart's shack. Vern was just waking up, and Froid peeked out of his shell.

Vern said, "Have you seen Herb the sharp shark? He might loan me his bus pass, and then we could go home." Bart said, "I think Groin the grey-green goat ate it. Maybe this little girl has one." Mark turned back the hands of his watch one more time, so he could be a boy again. No sooner did he have his shorts and his shirt back, than his watch broke. "Now how can we get back home?" he asked Vern. "I am almost starved to death." Vern said, "Well, you can fly if you try."

Soon Mark was back home, with a loaf and some milk for his lunch. His mum made him a lovely ham sandwich and a nice bowl of stew. Just as he was sitting down to eat, he felt a big sneeze coming. He pulled out his hankie, and his mum said,

"Why there is a picture of a vulture on your hankie. Where on earth did you get that?"

Do you think Mark is still hungry?

Word Search

Find the names of all the characters in the Froid stories

S	T	R	O	G	E	R	B	A	R	T
N	M	I	K	E	F	R	O	I	D	A
P	A	U	L	O	F	L	E	I	F	M
A	U	T	D	R	G	R	O	A	N	A
T	D	M	E	G	R	R	S	Y	E	N
C	H	A	A	E	E	V	O	Z	D	D
H	E	R	B	R	C	E	C	I	L	A
J	A	K	E	S	Y	V	E	R	N	E
H	A	N	K	U	D	A	W	N	K	L
Q	L	U	K	E	Z	P	N	E	A	L

Dancing Bears

Congratulations!
You have completed
Dancing Bears